"Stacee Reicherzer's book is a much-needec feelings of Otherness from a personal star into the material, but in a professional ma...... research and expertise. By presenting a path to help individuals overcome the fear that has governed their life, she opens up doors for those who have been excluded to walk into their full and authentic experience."

—**Tonya R. Hammer, PhD**, associate professor of counseling and counseling psychology, and Jennifer Jacques Flanery Community Counseling Professor at Oklahoma State University

"With wild anecdotes and heartfelt stories, Stacee Reicherzer speaks to every Other person out here. She not only provides actionable steps towards healing from bullying and ostracism, she does so with a wry humor that drew me in. The pages flew by as I laughed or cried at the shared memories all Othered people experience. Throughout this book, she brings some of the relational healing and community we so desperately need."

—**Adrian S. Warren, PhD, LPC-S**, president-elect of the Texas Counseling Association, and author of *Acceptance and Mindfulness for Healing and Recovery*

"Anyone who has ever felt different will benefit from this book, connecting with Stacee as she courageously shares her own experiences and those of people like us who have been Othered. You will feel that you are with a friend, counselor, teacher, and mentor, as she expertly guides you on a new journey of healing and growth."

—**John F. Marszalek III, PhD**, faculty of the clinical mental health counseling program at Southern New Hampshire University, and author of *Coming Out of the Magnolia Closet*

"This soulful love letter spoke to my heart and experiences of Otherness. As an African American woman, Stacee's artful language—like identifying your rock and laying down your burden—allowed me to recognize the spaces for my own restoration. This handbook gives us all pathways to clarity and freedom from internal and external oppressors, and it is an invitation to engage in exploration and healing with prescriptions worth taking."

—**Savitri Dixon-Saxon, PhD**, vice provost at Walden University, and North Carolina-licensed clinical mental health counselor

"This chef d'oeuvre was the perfect interruption to my isolation resulting from the COVID-19 pandemic. It fully satisfied my yearning for enlightenment and revived my creative spirit, consequently pulling it out of its cataclysmic quarantine. Suddenly, I was no longer alone as Stacee Reicherzer's soulfulness and unabashed sass unapologetically knocked on my door to take my mind, body, and soul on a swift and transformational journey of self-exploration and healing."

—**Fatma Salem, MA**, clinician at C.R.E.A.T.E! Center for Expressive Arts, Therapy and Education

"Reicherzer provides a compendium of behaviors and feelings contributing to the pain and difficulties of feeling Othered, with helpful remedies to heal that pain and grow into healthy, happy, and self-actualized people using personal creativity and sass. She speaks to many causes of the pain of Otherness with very constructive and pragmatic suggestions for the many suffering. She also gives practitioners new clinical insights into this important syndrome."

—**Edward S. Beck,** publisher and editor at *Kol Central PA*;
vice president of the Historic B'nai Jacob Synagogue
in Middletown, PA; and board member of the Jewish
Community Foundation of Central Pennsylvania

"The world has been telling us how to think and feel since the moment we entered it. That pressure—combined with taunts, slights, and abuses—creates a feeling of Otherness within us. Stacee Reicherzer has created a path for healing. The reader is guided gently—with compassion, love, and humor—through an exploration of the pain, shame, and guilt of feeling different in a world that values sameness."

—**Donna Sheperis, PhD**, professor of counseling at
Palo Alto University, and author of *Ethical Decision
Making for the 21st Century Counselor*

"With compassion, empathy, and an incredibly conversational tone, Reicherzer pulls you in with her uncanny ability to bring the trauma of Otherness to life. She gently guides the reader through user-friendly exercises of self-reflection, encouraging them to confront toxic aspects of dominant culture that dishonor and silence one's true self. This book is a must-have for anyone who wants to disrupt systemic oppression and finally belong."

—**Jada K. Hebra**, senior vice president and chief diversity and
inclusion officer at Southern New Hampshire University

"*The Healing Otherness Handbook* is just the medicine we needed at just the right time. In a world in which Othering hurts, harms, displaces, and creates trauma, Stacee Reicherzer invites the reader in to forge a path to healing to discover and claim our place at the table. Stacee's presence, wisdom, and humor remind the reader that she is walking with us on this journey, reminding us that our shared story of hurt can help us heal."

> **—Anne C. Deepak, PhD**, associate professor at the Monmouth University School of Social Work, and International Federation of Social Workers Representative to the United Nations

"Stacee Reicherzer is a model of resilience, bravery, intellect, and grace. Her book empowers me and will empower every reader to claim—without apology—the distinctive gifts he, she, or they have been given. Every day, Stacee helps to create the world in which I want to live, and, more important, the world in which I want our children to live—all of them."

> **—Chris Gilmer**, president and tenured professor of humanities at West Virginia University at Parkersburg, and founder of the National Institutes for Historically-Underserved Students

The Social Justice Handbook Series

As culture evolves, we need new tools to help us cope and interact with our social world in ways that feel authentic and empowered. That's why New Harbinger created the *Social Justice Handbook* series—a series that teaches readers how to use practical, psychology-based tools to challenge and transform dominant culture, both in their daily lives and in their communities.

Written by thought leaders in the fields of psychology, sociology, gender, and ethnic studies, the *Social Justice Handbook* series offers evidence-based strategies for coping with a broad range of social inequities that impact quality of life. As research has shown us, social oppression can lead to mental health issues such as depression, anxiety, trauma, lowered self-esteem, and self-harm. These handbooks provide accessible social analysis as well as thoughtful activities and exercises based on the latest psychological methods to help readers unlearn internalized negative messages, resist social inequities, transform their communities, and challenge dominant culture to be equitable for all.

The handbooks also serve as a hands-on resource for therapists who wish to integrate an understanding and acknowledgement of how multiple social issues impact their clients to provide relevant and supportive care.

For a complete list of books in
the *Social Justice Handbook* series,
visit newharbinger.com

THE
HEALING
OTHERNESS
HANDBOOK

OVERCOME THE **TRAUMA** OF
IDENTITY-BASED BULLYING & **FIND**
POWER IN **YOUR DIFFERENCE**

STACEE L. REICHERZER, PHD

New Harbinger Publications, Inc.

Publisher's Note

In consideration of evolving American English usage standards, and reflecting a commitment to equity for all genders, "they/them" is used in this book to denote singular persons.

NEW HARBINGER PUBLICATIONS is a registered trademark of New Harbinger Publications, Inc.

Distributed in Canada by Raincoast Books

Copyright © 2021 by Stacee Reicherzer
New Harbinger Publications, Inc.
5674 Shattuck Avenue
Oakland, CA 94609
www.newharbinger.com

Cover design by Sara Christian; Acquired by Georgia Kolias;
Edited by Jennifer Holder

MIX
Paper from
responsible sources
FSC® C011935
www.fsc.org

Library of Congress Cataloging-in-Publication Data

Names: Reicherzer, Stacee, author.
Title: The healing otherness handbook : overcome the trauma of identity-based bullying and find power in your difference / Stacee Reicherzer, PhD.
Description: Oakland, CA : New Harbinger Publications, Inc., 2021. | Series: The social justice handbook series | Includes bibliographical references.
Identifiers: LCCN 2020042547 (print) | LCCN 2020042548 (ebook) | ISBN 9781684036479 (trade paperback) | ISBN 9781684036486 (pdf) | ISBN 9781684036493 (epub)
Subjects: LCSH: Social isolation. | Other (Philosophy)--Psychological aspects. | Bullying.
Classification: LCC HM1131 .R45 2021 (print) | LCC HM1131 (ebook) | DDC 302.5/45--dc23
LC record available at https://lccn.loc.gov/2020042547
LC ebook record available at https://lccn.loc.gov/2020042548

Printed in the United States of America

23   22   21

10   9   8   7   6   5   4   3   2   1   First Printing

Contents

Introduction

I am a transgender woman and proud to be so. That's not something I could have said a few years ago. In fact, being proud of who I am still feels pretty new. Before, I didn't have the word "Other" to express what it is like to be cast out and condemned. As a gender nonconforming boy and later a transwoman, no word captured the pain of being called faggot, freak, or dude in a dress. Language failed my experiences of being assaulted, spat upon, isolated, exploited, cheated, harassed, discriminated against, and otherwise shut out. I couldn't articulate how walking down the street or entering a restaurant generated a weird, mixed feeling: on guard and hyperalert, ashamed and embarrassed by my differences, while attempting to appear unbothered. What's more, I couldn't describe what it's like to internalize someone else's denial of my right to be, and to use this as source material for self-loathing and shame. Nor did I have a word for the exhaustion I experienced as a result of all this.

Before I began my healing journey, within our gender-scripted society I believed I had to somehow prove that I deserved to be treated as a woman. Meanwhile, I denied my own hurt because I thought acknowledging it would be admitting weakness and giving in to people who hated me and tried to humiliate me. So I lied to myself, hoping that would convince Otherness to stop killing me inside. Because I held resentment and sadness but didn't have words to name the feelings, I Othered people who did things differently from me to gain a sense of control. I did not trust love that was given and attempted to rescue unhealthy people in an effort to prove…well, whatever I was trying to prove to myself each time I did it. Then I would realize my mistakes in hindsight and punish myself with shame for being queer and trans, inauthentic, cruel and angry, manipulative, and for rejecting people.

Healing took deep trauma work, beginning with the very first time I was cast as Other. Through the years, my journey involved facing and accepting my own reality, my own needs, my own rights. I used tools including meditation, exercises to grieve and forgive my past, and ways of tending the pain of Otherness. I created a path forward through dance, art, writing, and plenty of therapy. As a daily activity, I started to practice living a little more truth and becoming a little freer. I began to heal.

Now I have the words to describe my story of Otherness. I can articulate how this experience shows up in my own life and the lives of people with many different backgrounds. I now have tools I developed to shift the experience of being cast out as Other so it is no longer a self-definition. I no longer compare my life to see how much it resembles anyone else's—certainly not referencing people whose paths are not mine to walk. As a result, I no longer have shame driving my life choices, keeping me silent about who I am and what I need.

I now recognize that I deserve a place at the table, as do you. There's room at the table for all of us, despite what those who've bullied, harassed, oppressed, neglected, blamed, shamed, and otherwise harmed us would have us think. *We are all equal.* We all deserve to be here. This book can help you discover and claim your place.

I recognize that this book isn't going to erase or undo all the societal forms of Otherness that exist for you and that may threaten many aspects of your life and well-being. There are ways my life experience has been made possible through the legacy of Othering. My home state of Texas exists on the ancestral lands of Karankawa, Caddo, Apache, Comanche, Wichita, Coahuiltecan, Neches, Tonkawa, and many other Nations. The land became a part of Mexico before joining the United States, and its residents chose to side with the Confederacy in order to maintain an economic and social power structure built on the backs of enslaved Africans and their descendants. The sad stains of racial and ethnic Otherness continue to mark these places, through health and economic disparities that sometimes make the news, but more often are ignored.

This book is not going to end racism, misogyny, homohatred, ableism, antisemitism, islamophobia, transphobia, fat phobia, or anything else that people may still weaponize to try to force you down. It's not an attempt to compare social ills or build a false equivalence to explain different forms of oppression or social bullying. What you experienced is your own, and your story of Otherness doesn't require justification to be real to you. I am offering to help you free yourself from the messages you've internalized from these systems of oppression. That's what this work is about.

I wrote this book while visualizing an imagined reader in front of me. Sometimes she was a single mom returning to college in an effort to make a better life for herself and her family. Other times, I saw a young person coming out into the LGBTQ world and trying to answer the questions surrounding "Who am I?" I also wrote to a person trying to understand and heal not only their own story, but also their ancestors' generational Otherness trauma. In this visualization, I imagined so many faces and voices all engaged in a healing circle with me as I wrote this book for you—to your face and voice.

I hope you'll consider creating a healing reading circle to navigate this book together. Such circles are an ancient means for coming to a shared understanding of an experience like Otherness and using the power of group experience to lift each other up. There is power in creating spaces with people who have a vested interest in personal growth. For this reason, I created several guides to accompany this book. Therapists can find resources for individual and group healing online at http://www.newharbinger.com/46479. If you are interested in journeying with a circle of people, take a look at the Reading Group Guide I offer at the end of the book.

With that said, let's get your healing journey started.

PART 1

YOUR DECISION TO NO LONGER LIVE SMALL

CHAPTER 1

A Kid Who Was "Different"

If you have spent much time feeling like an outsider, you know exactly how lonely it can be. We've all had the experience of walking into a crowded room and being the only person of our kind, whatever that meant: our generation, our gender, our racial or ethnic group, our profession. In these instances, perhaps we were only temporary outsiders...and whatever worry we had about our difference quickly abated after spotting a friend, finding someone equally nervous, discovering something in common, or having a drink or two or five to gain liquid courage for social interaction. But for many of us, feeling like an outsider in a crowded room, like an Other, has been our life story.

We were the kids who were different—whatever "different" meant—and we felt it whenever we stepped out, into the world. There were good reasons for this: sometimes we were ostracized for our obvious differences, sometimes we were bullied for arbitrary reasons, sometimes we just carried a strange feeling that we didn't fit in. Whatever the cause for this feeling of being Other, it formed a deep and pervasive childhood trauma that we're still carrying with us today. Yes, the fact that the experience of being cast out led to a belief that we are less-than, unworthy, stupid, inferior, ugly, or undeserving, is indeed a form of trauma.

There is a spectrum of experiences that can be termed Other, from the deeply entrenched injustice of systemic racism and sexism to the more individual forms of rejection that are based on some slight perceived difference or inadequacy. For some of us, Otherness comes from messages we were given because of our culture or religion, our sexual or gender identity and expression, or aspects of our appearance that suggested our class positions relative to those with the power, money, and guns to silence us. Some were cast out as Other based on our neurology and how we processed information in a way that others thought made us crazy, a nuisance, or stupid. Sometimes, it was aspects of our body: its shape and appearance, how we moved, saw, or heard in the world around us...or how we did not.

Wherever we happen to fall within this spectrum, whatever the cause for being made to feel different and judged and shamed, to live as Other can be isolating and even terrifying. Being cast out as Other in a society that doesn't entirely accept us, understand us, or respond to us for who we are—or responds with hate toward some aspect of our being—can make us feel less than equal. Through this book, I will guide you to release the trauma that's still within you through others' bullying, belittling, and rejection, so you can find power in the qualities that make you *You* and let go of fear in order to live fully.

When we are ruled by fear of rejection, silencing, and even violent oppression, we become so accustomed to those possibilities that we allow toxic conditions to shape our beliefs about ourselves and what we can or cannot do. We create *rules of fear* to survive. Maybe we're told, "I don't like the ways you're different, and you'd better tone it down" so often that we eventually start telling ourselves the same thing whenever behaviors that make us Other threaten to come out. Another message we might hear, and internalize as a rule, is: "You'll have to work twice as hard, considering how inadequate you are." Or, "You shouldn't complain—others are worse off than you." And sometimes the rule we internalize is "Oh, I shouldn't still be feeling resentful"—even when resentful feelings are a normal and very human response to the mistreatment we're facing. Finally, we arrive at the cruelest rule of all, for it reflects our sense of hopelessness to transform ourselves or society: "I cannot change the world."

Dysfunctional as all these rules seem, they help us survive being cast out as Other. Survival is, after all, something we do even in very toxic conditions. Like fish swimming in dirty brown aquarium water that's thick with algae, we adapt to the climate of oppression. After all, people who've benefited from our oppression are in charge. If someone gets around to feeding us in our sad little fish tanks, we'll take whatever can be spared, maybe even convincing ourselves that we should feel grateful for it. We even start treating these conditions like they're normal.

Little by little, these old survival messages from our past have become the scripted rules for our present. They start to shape every aspect of how we think and act in different parts of our lives as parents, partners, and professionals. When we engage the world through our rules of fear and the heavily edited versions of our selves that result, we fail to capitalize on the power of possibility. This happens no matter how successful we are in our career, no matter how beautiful our home, children, and lives seem to otherwise be. We question why we feel so unhappy when these things "should" bring us joy. Over time, this existence becomes habitual. We stymie the dreamer, the lover, the artist, the knower. Instead, we let fear establish rules that construct a glass box for us to live in and that fill it with muck.

What if I told you that instead of continuing to feel self-conscious, inadequate, measured, and edited by an external rule maker, you can love that thing about you that's your own? You no longer need to be ruled by fear and somebody else's script for your life. I will teach you to recognize and claim your strength, roar with it, and live with it as a guiding truth that encourages you to do that next right thing for yourself. There is so much more to life than swimming around in our own muck. There is a big, bold, audacious life ahead.

I know it feels hard because so much is out in the world, which you cannot control. But together we are going to do whatever is needed so that you no longer allow your external oppressors to be the internal voice that tells you "You cannot..." Under that shame, doubt, and fear lives a choicemaker, a *You* who is able to make choices and take bold action toward what you want, need, and deserve.

In this book, I have mapped a journey that will take you past the muck of fear-based shame to show you all the essential beauty and depth of spirit that make up the dreamer, the thinker, the feeler, and the creator who knows exactly what you must do to feel fulfilled.

Your Journey to Freedom

You're on a journey to freedom. In the chapters to come, you'll explore your Otherness story: how it began, ways it has affected you, and how you coped up to this point. Then you'll learn tools to deal with this story differently, primarily through breathing and meditation. These allow you to contact who you are now, beyond the self-doubt and self-punishing thoughts and memories of Otherness. You will feel compassion for yourself and even gratitude for the strength to overcome obstacles and learn lessons along the way. A fresh creativity will arise for finding new, life-enhancing ways to replace the fear-based thinking that created the obstacles of the past. And sass will give you permission to be bold in the pursuit of your life vision, free from the roles that Otherness led you to assume.

As anyone who's made a courageous life change can attest, a life of freedom is both exciting and terrifying. Fear-based rules are strong, so as you embark on whatever spiritual, emotional, or physical journey you must undertake, you may fear isolation and wonder, "Who will remain with me and who will abandon ship?" Yet, as you make the courageous decision to no longer be ruled by fear and instead choose the freedom of having an authentic voice, you'll attract people who are also making the courageous choice to live their truth. In the LGBTQ community, we use "family of choice" to signify those we choose, and who've chosen us, as family. Trust that your freedom will guide you to find your own family of choice.

The decision to live free doesn't only impact you, it will inspire others as well. You'll parent your children by teaching them to trust, rather than dull, their instincts for survival and you'll stop filling their heads with your own fears. You'll inspire people in your community—the neighborhood, workplace, or however "community" is defined by you—with your willingness to live your life exactly as you are. And you'll learn to cherish others for their differences in an expanding circle of appreciation for human diversity.

The journey to freedom comes with sacrifices, and certainty is one of the first things to go. It's natural to fear what will happen when you face old hurts that you've tried to ignore. Yet, at no point during the journey are you required to do something that doesn't feel authentic to your spirit. To the contrary, this is a book for building an understanding of your authenticity so you can find your way to live with it. By exploring each rule in your life and how it tends to show up, then taking steps to dismantle the rule and free yourself of its harmful message, you'll practice a way of living that reflects your yearnings for a truer existence. Ultimately, the price you've paid for certainty is that you gave up this call to find the freedom to truly be yourself. There's still a yearning to be yourself, the whole *You* that is inside, which will now be awakened and given voice.

I don't promise a life that will suddenly be easy. I do promise that by following the journey to freedom, now and as a continued practice, you won't spend your final days wondering, "What if?" I promise that freedom, while scary as hell at times, is better than the certainty of an unhappy life that somebody else laid out for you.

How Otherness May Show Up for You

I invite you to think for a moment about the areas of your life in which you've been treated differently or "less than." What has it meant to move through life being the person you are? Even if an item listed here isn't a source of Othering in your present reality, think about how you may have experienced it in the past. Breathe deeply and allow your mind to drift into each different part of your experience. As you review these aspects of identity and parts of being, think about each one and reflect on how people have treated you in response.

- Your gender—the roles and expectations people had for you as a girl or a boy, and later as a woman, man, or person living in the transgender spectrum

- Your racial or ethnic background—the limits that people placed on who you could be or what you might be capable of achieving, the qualities they think you possess based on what they saw (or mistook) about you

- Your sexual identity—who you love, whether women, men, transpeople, or some delightful combination of these

- Your physical mobility—how people have perceived you and labeled your movement through the world, determining what you could or could not do as a result

- How you learn and process information—how you read, complete math, are able to stay focused, or how you present ideas and things you discover

- Your body's size, shape, or appearance—the labels people assign you, the assumptions they make about you and how you live, their determining whether you are attractive and dateable

- Your family's faith tradition—the role that religion and spirituality play in your life, as it may differ from the dominant belief systems around you

- Your family's economic situation—the side of the tracks you live on, the shoes you wear, the lunch your family can afford...or not afford

To delve further, in addition to the Otherness we experience in society, many of us were cast as Other within our own families. Perhaps you were treated as an outsider in your childhood home. Maybe you were the only one in the schoolyard, workplace, and other spaces you occupied to experience your family's level of chaos. You may have been abused for your differences—emotionally, physically, even sexually—and still carry the belief that you're somehow responsible for these violations against your body and spirit.

These wounds are often the most difficult to heal because when your caregivers are the ones who isolate, abuse, or scapegoat you, you're raised believing that this is the norm you should expect throughout life. What's more, you experienced much of this at an age when you were too young to do anything about it. Those who might have helped you either weren't in a position to do so or weren't willing to interfere. This may result in these kinds of Otherness.

- Your family treated your individual goals and qualities, which differed from their own, as flawed and "less than."

- You were compared to a sibling, cousin, neighbor, or someone else in your community whose qualities you could not possess, even if you tried.

- Your family expected you to keep their secrets from the outside world and pretend you weren't seeing the things you witnessed.

- You were the resented child of a parent who left the household in which you were raised.

- Your family was more concerned about how the outside world perceived you as a representation of them than about your actual needs.

Many of our experiences of Otherness sit below our conscious awareness. You may not think of these things much in your day-to-day life. After all, we grew up to move along with our lives and whatever choices we made, didn't we? But it's likely that the wounds of Otherness that were inflicted in childhood still get reopened and salted—often when you don't expect it. As a final part to this assessment, consider how many of these points are true for you, in your present life.

- You often enter situations expecting rejection.

- You feel like an imposter in one or more areas of your life.

- You still experience painful feelings whenever you spend time with your family, in your hometown, or around people who remind you of the culture you grew up in.

- You are still working to prove that you matter and have worth, whether to your family, your community, or some other entity that you can't understand or name.

- You experience fear or helpless rage when you see others who share your gender, race, sexual identity, or other characteristics, undergo oppression, abuse, or are treated as second-class citizens.

- You still doubt your ability to soar, make waves, have an impact, and follow your dreams.

As you considered these statements, you may have encountered difficult feelings and memories. This is normal. Just keep in mind that by reading this book, you're going on a journey to build strength and clarity. At the moment, heavy stuff is still keeping you in a negative headspace about your inadequacy, your lack of worth, and your lack of control. In my work with Otherness over the last several years, I've learned these seven central truths about the experience.

1. Being ostracized, bullied, discriminated against, and forgotten about as a child is a form of shame-based trauma.

2. Otherness trauma instills a great deal of fear.

3. Fear doesn't just go away because we grow up. Rather, it drives home certain false rules that we follow into adulthood.

4. The rules of fear show up in many ways throughout our lives, influencing what we believe about ourselves and how we participate in relationships.

5. Like other forms of trauma, the trauma of Otherness can be healed.

6. As we heal from our sense of Otherness, we can follow a path of mental, emotional, and spiritual freedom.

7. When we learn to recognize our distinct life path and experience the vast wonder of our spirit in many dimensions, we can create the life that we deserve.

Going to the Roots of Otherness

Our memory networks function like the banyan tree, which has a single large trunk surrounded by aerial roots. These roots spring from the branches, find their way to the ground, and burrow in, eventually growing larger to become trunks themselves. In time, a single banyan tree appears as a grove of interconnected trees. Similarly, our memory networks cause one memory to branch off into a host of associated sensations, feelings, thoughts, and other memories.

Think of a pivotal experience that took place at an earlier time in your life: perhaps your first love, coming out, the birth of your child, or moving out of your parents' home. Spend a few minutes experiencing the images that come to mind, the emotions that accompany the memory, and any bodily sensations you might feel. By doing this, you've accessed a memory network, a banyan tree of information that has likely played a pivotal role in your development. It has shaped how you think and act as you participate in different roles and responsibilities like partnering, parenting, managing and paying your bills, maintaining a household, and more.

Our experiences of being cast out as Other also impact us this way. However, because we typically experienced Otherness for the first time during childhood, our memories reside at a deeper level than adult memories. Our brains develop rapidly during childhood, allowing us to take in the experiences of the world with progressive levels of understanding that unfold quickly. This is why a child who's first learning words to describe the world might call all four-legged and furry animals at the zoo "dog." At first, they may seem to resemble the family's terrier, but within a few months a child can distinguish the zebras, lions, and bears as distinct species.

The brain's adaptive nature during childhood also means that beliefs about yourself become very easily ingrained. If as an eight-year-old child you were told that you're ugly, stupid, or otherwise flawed, it had a significant impact because your understanding of yourself was in a period of rapid development. The negative experience became part of your memories, forming a network that grew more robust each time you took in another harmful message that reinforced what you had been told.

During our formative years as children, we don't simply hear the words and feel the fists that tell us we are Other, we *learn* these words and fists so they become part of how we understand ourselves. We take in messages that we are less worthy than others, and we *believe* them. As we grow into adulthood, we learn to act in response. For example, you might have figured out that people eventually tire of hurting you, so you allow them to continue by pretending it doesn't matter. Or perhaps you ease your emotions by inflicting pain on someone younger and smaller. These actions are in response to distress and also become part of your memory network.

Here's another thing the analogy of the banyan tree teaches us: if we can speak truthfully about the first time we knew we were Other, we can hit the heart of the grove and the network of hurt that springs from it. This is where our work begins.

Recalling Your First Experience as Other

I first felt Otherness when I was eight years old and was called a faggot. I was riding my bike toward the swings where the neighborhood kids played when school was out. As I peddled there, I saw an older boy I recognized because he went to school with my stepsister. He was with two other boys that I recognized but didn't know.

I don't remember which one of them was the first to call me a fag, but I will never forget the fear I felt when I heard the word used against me. I didn't know what it meant, but everything about the way they said it told me that it was awful, vile, detestable. The word got louder: "Fag! Fag! FAG!" I realized quickly that the swings were a dangerous place to be on that summer day.

"Get out of here, fag!" they yelled, and as I peddled away they hurled large clumps of black South Texas dirt, clayish, wet, and heavy. My memory of the event fades with an image of riding, terrified, back to the safety of home. "FAG! FAGGOT!" The words tore into me.

In the days and weeks that followed, my sense that something was wrong with me continued to grow. But I couldn't put my finger on or describe precisely what was wrong with me. It was confusing because I didn't understand what "fag" meant or why it applied to me. When those kids looked at me, they saw a feminine little boy whose behavior was more typical of girls. Gender nonconformity wasn't tolerated for little boys growing up in the 1970s, and this was the only word they knew to tell me that I was not like them and never would be.

In the years that followed, I was called a fag many times, steadily feeding isolation, confusion, fear, and sadness that lasted throughout my adolescence. Otherness continued, even years after my transgender journey was completed. In response, I lived the rules of fear fully.

Now it's your turn to look back. That first moment you were cast as Other may be difficult to immediately recall. It's embedded in a bank of memories that jumble together and may be confusing. If your Otherness story involves serious trauma, your brain may block the memory entirely from your awareness, manifesting it in other symptoms that disrupt your life. Go with what you have.

Keep in mind that recalling a memory does not require that you dwell on it. The exercise that follows allows you to view your memory from a safe distance and repurpose the memory as something you can overcome.

ARRIVE AT THE ROOT OF OTHERNESS

Once you've established this first memory of Otherness in your consciousness, we'll begin the task of addressing it. I invite you to "float back" into the past by following these steps (Shapiro 2001; adapted with permission).

1. Think about the part of your life which, for as long as you can remember, has made you feel most like an outsider. Whatever it happens to be, breathe deeply and allow your mind to drift to this part of your experience.

2. Notice the body sensations that arise. Maybe you feel a tightness in your chest or shoulders, or even a sensation of nausea. Whatever you feel, simply notice it.

3. Notice the emotions that accompany this experience. You may feel a little low, sad, or maybe angry. Perhaps you feel foggy and confused. Just notice your emotions without judgement.

4. Listen for a message that accompanies these sensations and emotions, which may express as something like, "I am lazy," "I am ugly," "I am stupid." Whatever belief comes to you is the one we're attempting to isolate.

5. Next, close your eyes, take a few deep breaths, and let your mind drift naturally and unforced to the first time you experienced these sensations and feelings, the initial moment you received the negative message. You may picture a clear event or a fuzzy series of images with no specific details.

6. If you are able to do so, write a short description of what you recall from that day and its aftermath in the period that followed. Your ability to write the story of the event is a truth-telling exercise. This act gives you control over the moment and begins the process of bringing the incident to light.

Let's pause to acknowledge the tremendous courage you possess. Glancing back at these memories and exploring their impact on your life takes bravery. While you may be able to clearly label encounters from your life as cruel, degrading, sexist, racist, or phobic, you're now on a journey to heal lingering hurt. It's one thing to identify an experience as unjust, but quite another to begin repairing your spirit from what this harm, and every other social injustice, has done to you. This is what bravery looks like. We'll continue our exploration of the impacts of Otherness in chapter 2.

Our shared story of hurt can help us heal. The details of our stories vary a great deal. Yet, even as they differ, our stories strike similar themes. In each, there is the disruption, confusion, and shaming of a child. Each time, this occurred as a result of some person or group with power, both real and perceived, casting us as Other. The shadow of childhood experiences of Otherness linger into adulthood, in spite of whatever life gains each of us make. Throughout this book, I'll share stories because we can heal together. Hold space for your story as you read about Eddie and Jeanette.

Eddie's Story

Eddie was never able to recall a time in his life when he didn't have
excess weight. Shy by nature but otherwise friendly and easygoing,
Eddie had a small circle of friends during his elementary school years.

While other children did tease him, it never felt excessive or extremely isolating.

That changed when he reached middle school. As he reached puberty, Eddie's body mass pushed into obesity. It wasn't long before he started hearing taunts whenever he undressed in the gym locker room: "Jabba," "pig," "fat ass." These escalated to physical torment, with boys grabbing and twisting his nipples and forcefully jabbing his stomach. When the boys picked their teams for gym activities, Eddie was always chosen last.

The boys who had been Eddie's friends throughout elementary school began to separate from him, worried for their own social capital. Eventually, Eddie found himself eating lunch by himself every day. The taunts, jokes at his expense, and isolation were hallmarks of his remaining years at school. What's more, as kids in school began dating, Eddie's shyness around girls kept him from ever pursuing relationships with them, even friendships. This continued well into his adulthood.

Eddie's social isolation impacted his self-esteem, and he spent years trying crash diets and other extreme efforts to lose weight, none of which yielded lasting results. He gained all of his weight back. Eddie chose to live alone and made no attempts to date, fearing that his efforts to engage in relationships with women would invariably lead to rejection. He continued to be cast as Other by airline passengers when traveling for work (including a woman who berated him for "spilling into" her seat), by fellow grocery shoppers who glanced into his basket to assess his food choices, and by people staring then rapidly averting their gaze. He pretended not to notice so they didn't feel uncomfortable.

In spite of people's mistreatment of him, Eddie worked hard to maintain a cheery disposition. At times, he even colluded with their cruelty and made fat jokes about himself. Inwardly, he wasn't really experiencing humor. Instead, he was trying to deflect people's aggression toward him, believing that if he made them laugh, they would like him. Jokes that degrade him were a form of coping with the ongoing experience of Otherness.

One of the many terrible lessons that Otherness teaches us is that we must apologize to people for the space we take up in the world, while silencing the hurt that comes from years of injustice. Jeanette's story illustrates this further with its themes of shame, grief, and anger.

Jeanette's Story

Jeanette was born to a loving African American family who doted on her, encouraging her academic talent and athleticism. She lived the first thirteen years of her life with her parents and two sisters in a culturally diverse East Coast community. When Jeannette was in eighth grade, her father was promoted and her family moved to Arizona. Her life changed.

One of only five Black students in an otherwise predominantly White school, Jeanette knew that she stood out from most of the other kids. Though her parents had foreseen the difficulties of her new school and spoke to Jeanette about the need to present herself with confidence, she still felt uncertain of her role there. Jeanette found the other Black students were friendly enough, but she had trouble relating to them as her East Coast experiences and cultural reference points were very different from theirs. Her greatest struggles resulted from her interactions with the White students. None seemed overtly hostile, but most ignored her. Those who did pay attention to her seemed patronizing, asking if they could touch her hair or whether it was hard to find makeup for her skin.

The moment Jeanette recalled when she floated back to the first time she was cast as Other was when a teacher showed Gone with the Wind in American History class. Things got worse for Jeanette after that. The other kids began asking her intrusive questions about the African American characters' speech and behaviors in the movie, particularly in Butterfly McQueen's role as Prissy. Jeannette felt alone, isolated, and humiliated by having to engage these students. She also experienced a deeper wounding by seeing her own ancestral trauma as an African American caricaturized in a movie that was shown by her teacher as an accurate depiction of American History during the Civil War.

When Jeanette first presented the issues to her mother, Lorna, she was told, "This is how the world is and you'll always have to deal with ignorance. Keep your chin up and never let them see that they're bothering you." As Jeanette later learned and came to understand through adult eyes, her parents were grappling with their own challenges integrating into a community with very few Black families. Lorna had worried about making matters worse for Jeannette if she voiced her concerns to the school. Nonetheless, Jeanette took her mother's advice, "chinning up" to the school environment and pouring herself into her grades. As she recounted in her adult years, this period was marked by continuous exhaustion, helpless anger, and a sense of loss and abandonment.

Now, with a family of her own dependent on her and as a humanities scholar, Jeanette has spent years working to prove she is a smart and competent professional, but often with a paradox. The "chin up" message has stayed with her, but she finds it put to the test when she encounters microaggressions in her workplace, like being asked to participate on diversity committees as a representative woman of color, being paid much less than White male colleagues, and having her research contributions overlooked. Jeanette has suffered from anxiety and hypertension as she doubles down on her professional efforts to remain always poised and professional lest she be cast as an "angry Black woman." Her duties as a parent, with the added stress of raising two sons who Jeanette worries will be targeted for skin color, leave her feeling "constantly on display to a world that's waiting for me to mess up." Jeannette acknowledges that she frequently eats her feelings and overspends money.

As you embark on the journey of uncovering past and enduring portions of your life that have caused untold pain and disruption, it's normal to feel scared, isolated, and vulnerable about the task. Chances are you've tried very hard to forget and move on from these difficult memories.

Even as you've grown older, the painful ordeal of your childhood experiences of Otherness remain a filter through which you experience the world. For those who've experienced deep ancestral trauma, like Jeanette, the wounds from your ancestors' Otherness is with you also. None of us chose the circumstances in which we've been cast out as Other, and your ancestors most certainly didn't choose theirs. Nor do we choose the ongoing forces of oppression and conflict that seem ever-present in much of the world today.

We do have the power to make a conscious choice not to allow shame to dictate how we respond to these circumstances. We have the power to see muck from outside of us for what it is, and to forge new internal beliefs about who we are and what we can do that aren't tainted by ways others have shamed us.

CHAPTER 2

What Rejection Does to Us

Let's do a quick experiment. I'm going to ask you to bring to mind two memories. No need to dwell for long on either…just recall it, then let it pass. Ready? The first is this: remember a time when you banged your shin. Chances are, the memory is vivid enough to make you wince as you recall the pain, and probably includes the setting in which the incident occurred.

Next, recall a time when some person or group excluded you, whether purposefully or not. Bringing the memory to mind, you probably experience a moment of pain in the form of sadness or other emotions. Like the memory of banging your shin, the memory of exclusion is painful, and the details and people involved also come to mind.

Both the physical pain of banging your shin and the social pain of being excluded appear to be processed in the same regions of the brain. As you read the stories of Otherness in chapter 1 and related your own experience, you may have felt any number of emotions such as sadness and helpless rage. You may have felt confusion over unanswered questions like "Why did they hate me?" or "Why didn't anyone see that I was in pain?" Whatever hurt that lingers from these experiences is as real and valid as pain you have from memories of physical injuries (Eisenberger, Lieberman, and Williams 2003; Sleegers, Proulx, and Van Beest 2016). In other words, it literally hurts to feel left out. That's helpful for you to know next time someone suggests you should get past a social incident, which they may call "trivial," that actually hurt you.

Just as physical injuries teach us a thing or two about safety around stoves, driving a car, or dancing next to sharply cornered coffee tables and bedframes (my thing), memories of socially painful experiences have also shaped us. We learn from social rejection that certain people and circumstances are to be avoided. Over time we even develop hunches about social situations—that we'll be humiliated somehow, our humanity attacked or simply not recognized—and these cause us to withdraw. For many people, this is the basis of social anxiety.

The forms of rejection that hurt the most are often the ones that reflect our original experiences of being cast as Other. In adulthood, our Otherness story is reawakened in life situations like breakups or being turned down for a job. We also feel alone and exposed when we're a newcomer in a city, job, school, or even a party where we don't know anyone. In such moments, suddenly all of those old feelings of exclusion and feeling like an outsider return. This intense separation and aloneness come with a belief that in our differentness we are somehow inferior, less smart, less capable, less together (whatever "together" means). It suddenly shows up and we feel like we're ten or twelve or sixteen years old again. Those familiar rules of fear and painful core beliefs bubble up, and we default to the same coping mechanisms.

However, if we can dig into experiences and memories that caused these old wounds of exclusion and rejection, we can begin to heal those wounds and learn new ways of engaging the world. To get going on this path, I'll share how memory works and we'll explore what makes some experiences—like your memories of Otherness—stand out.

Exploring Your Otherness Memories

Most of what happens in life is fairly routine. The aspects of environments and experiences that our brains recognize as typical fall to the background in our awareness so that we can focus on things that require concentration. If you drive to work each day for five years, your brain will remember the drive but not each specific instance. Only those drives in which something unexpected happened would stick in your memory.

Similarly, imagine taking out the trash one day, the way you had for years, only to see a giraffe walk out from behind your neighbor's house to stick its tongue out at you. You'd remember a lot of specifics surrounding this event, such as the weather or whatever dinner you just placed in the oven, that you'd never recall from any ordinary time you took out the trash. You'd remember the sight of the giraffe: the details of its markings and feeling absolutely shocked when it appeared. What's more, from that point on, you might start looking for giraffes anytime you walk out of your house.

This is how memory works. Things that aren't typical stick. Trauma memories, including Othering, stay with us because they're such an abrupt break from what's typical for us in a given context. If the first time you recall feeling bullied or erased was in third grade, you'll remember that event precisely for how it stands out from the rest of your third-grade experience. Whereas you might otherwise have general memories of your class—your teacher, where your classroom was, and what you enjoyed eating for lunch—the Otherness memory stands out just as the giraffe memory would. This jarring experience created a strong emotional reaction like surprise, fear, hurt, or whatever else happened within your third-grade self. Later, you'd recall a mixture of mental pictures, perhaps even sounds and smells. If you had a bodily reaction like vomiting, you may recall that too.

If your Otherness memory occurred in your home, the memory would stand out from whatever your normal routine was there. A shaming event at the dinner table would be recalled along with whatever meal was served, who was at the table, and other details of the story. You'd also recall the sadness, anger, confusion, and particular body sensations you had then—which you may experience even now. Otherness memories within family life are particularly potent because they often come with someone's insistence that you're too sensitive, too emotional, too whatever—as if it's your fault you're hurting. Some of us still believe this.

Children's brains are extremely malleable, which is why kids quickly learn languages, how to program their grandparents' smartphones, or anything they're taught. Children also learn to navigate a world of safe and unsafe relationships with the same level of adaptive skill. When children live among cruel people, they learn the survival skills that are required in order to exist in these circumstances.

How a Trauma Memory Is Stored and Later Relived

Going back to the memory of banging your shin, a memory network formed from the first time you did it. This happens in service to the body, to prevent us from wrecking our shin bones. If we didn't have the memory of our pain, we'd continually reinjure ourselves. In much the same way, memories of situations that were emotionally painful form to protect us from the danger that we perceived at the time.

If you were bullied as a child, you learned a whole map of the school in order to avoid bullies. If you were different from your family in some way, and that difference was denigrated in your home, you learned how to appease, avoid, or numb yourself to abusers or neglectors. The memories that formed were to keep you safe. In later years, when you encountered experiences that felt an awful lot like bullying or isolation, that old memory network lit up like a Christmas tree, guiding you toward familiar actions for dealing with the perceived hurt or danger.

It can be easiest to see how this works with memories of love and safety, which form anchors to powerful memory networks that guide us when we experience these feelings in our relationships. Try this: Bring to mind a person who feels especially safe. Picture the person fully and breathe this image in. The memory networks associated with that person are now activated. What's physically going on is a series of neural impulses: your mental picture of the person, the sound of their voice, associated smell and touch sensations. You'll also notice warm feelings that come with safety, like contentment, joy, or playfulness. Maybe a thought like "I love you!" is also present. You may experience a relaxed sensation through-out your body. Sadness may follow if this person is no longer with you. This is the longing that's associated with memory.

Next, bring to mind a person who feels unsafe. Immediately, you'll notice the shift in your body as whatever mental picture you have of the person comes into focus. You may bristle at a memory of this person's voice and experience uncomfortable feelings such as anger, sadness, or fear. Your thoughts may be equally strong: "You betrayed my trust," "You hated me for no reason," "You never accepted me."

See how this works? When you brought these contrasting individuals to mind, you experienced two vastly different reactions, both of which are entirely based on the mental images you carry with all of the feelings, body sensations, and thoughts associated with them. This is how memory is relived.

Things like songs or the feel of the air at a certain time of year connect us with memories that are pleasant or unpleasant. Emotions are also reflections of memories. We know what joy is because we've felt it before and recognize it whenever we have it again. What's more, we seek the people or situations that bring us joy and avoid those that do not. Often the process doesn't use much conscious thought. No one's ever said to someone they're falling in love with, "Not only do I enjoy you and the cool things about you, but you make me feel safe like my grandmother used to!" It kind of kills the moment. To the brain, these feelings of safety with Grandma are what we've learned to associate with love.

Fortunately, we don't have to do this level of thinking. Memory and its associated feelings, like safety with Grandma, do the heavy lifting for us. It's a similar mechanism at play when an Otherness memory is recalled. Each time the brain perceives circumstances that feel similar to being cast out as Other, it moves into action with all of the accompanying emotions, thoughts, and actions. In many cases, the exact memory of Otherness isn't apparent to us in the moment. We don't consciously think things like, "Wow, this breakup feels a whole lot like rejection. It takes me back to that time in fourth grade." We just find ourselves reacting to particular people and social situations without realizing why.

How We Perceive Rejection

When encountering people whose behavior looks and feels a lot like exclusion, we make the mental jump to our story of Otherness and go with "They don't like me because I'm different." This can even happen to us when we're not being purposefully excluded. We feel like outsiders even in routine social situations, as anyone who's been to a party attended by strangers can attest. Even extremely social people struggle in these instances. The thought process goes something like this: "Okay, I don't know anyone at this party. New kid on the block again. Hope I'm not the only person like me here. Oh, they're staring at me. This blouse doesn't look good on me, does it? I knew I should have worn the blue one. I'm doing that nervous laugh thing again! Wow, that was really loud. How soon can I leave?"

Here's what is really happening in this scenario. The brain is rapidly firing messages that we're essentially unsafe in the new situation. The brain adapted this response from past experiences, such as situations where we were actually unsafe or being judged on the very things that we're now hyperconsciously self-criticizing: our clothes, our laugh, some aspect of our body, our culture, or a style of personal expression that's different.

For those of us whose stories as Other have been constant and are embedded, we're never unaware of our differences. In fact, we're so painfully aware of our differences that we sometimes go into situations anticipating rejection that's not intended. How often do we personalize the brusque treatment of a store clerk or waitperson without considering the personal stressors, like a sick child or car trouble, that may be distracting them? How often do we assume, like at the party I just described, that the people there are rejecting us? They're more likely experiencing their own fears and insecurities as well. This can lead us to reject the situation before it rejects us.

Because our memories of Otherness are so painful and powerful, and our circumstances reinforce those messages, we allow fear to creep in. We create distance and isolation to keep ourselves safe. This takes us deeper down the well until we're drowning in sorrow and silence. None of this is helpful, for isolation is the most damaging tool we can use against ourselves.

Instead, what if we make the decision to understand our fear and refuse to be ruled by it? We can actively work to recognize and rebut the thoughts that lead to the downward spiral. This requires us to distinguish those things that truly ostracize and oppress us—and oh, these social biases do exist—from the things that we create in our own minds. Then we can decide what we will do with both experiences. The key here is to recognize ourselves as choicemakers in response to fear of rejection. We can own our decision-making process to live and love as fully as we can.

RECALLING A POWERFUL CHOICE

It's powerful to recognize the agency we have, the choicemaking that's already taking place in our lives—with particular attention to the times when fear did *not* win. Consider an adult experience of a choice you made turning out unexpectedly well for you. Perhaps you chose a relationship, a job, or a new city and found that it improved your life. Maybe you decided to complete a college degree or start going to the gym. It could be a new religious institution, social gathering place, or foreign country where you didn't know the culture. You may have heard all sorts of inner alarms and were quite certain that things would not go well—yet you made it through and things went well. As you imagine the situation, grab something to record your thoughts, whether a pen and paper, laptop, or smartphone. Then pay particular attention to the following:

- The mental picture you had, prior to the experience, of what you thought would happen.

- The beliefs you held about the situation, like "They'll never choose me," "They're going to look down on me," "I'll be all by myself and no one will talk to me." Write whatever was real for you.

- The feelings that came up for you in response to this thought, whether sadness, anger, loneliness, or any emotion. All feelings are valid.

- The place in your body that gets your attention as you recall this memory. Is anything tingling, buzzing, warm, or hurting?

- What made it possible for you to proceed in spite of your fears? Specifically, write down what you drew from as a source of strength and courage that allowed you to make the choice to show up as you did. Maybe it was an inspirational saying, advice from a mentor, or a strong desire driving you.

You can celebrate that you didn't give in. While the fear of rejection was there, *you didn't let it stop you.* Instead, you showed up for the life event by choice and it turned out well for you.

We cannot allow the fear of rejection to keep us from showing up. Surmounting our fear begins by trusting that when we bring our full, authentic selves into a situation, we invite acceptance. When we expect to be treated with respect and to be welcomed, we shift the game. A space is created in which we're able to act more freely—oftentimes with others responding positively to our sense of freedom. Even if others don't respond and remain trapped in their internalized social narratives that dictate the kind of people that they and others "should" be, we can enter situations with self-compassion and acceptance. This way, we navigate the situation and the people in it with resiliency, secure in our inherent self-worth even during those times when perfect acceptance is not what we find.

To find our way toward living with the freedom and sense of wholeness we deserve as our birthright, we must overcome the rules of fear. These have been learned through our experiences of Otherness and led to this chronic expectation of rejection. Let's consider each of the five rules of fear that Otherness instills, examining how each manifests even years after the experiences took place. In part two of this book, I'll share how to free yourself from each one.

Rule 1: "You Shouldn't Complain Because Others Are Worse Off Than You"

This rule exists to keep us from acknowledging our pain and our trauma from being cast out as Other. It does so by teaching us we're supposed to believe "things aren't really *that* bad"—implying that the pain we feel isn't real or doesn't matter.

This is a fascinating moral that most of us learned from an early age. Middleclass, White kids in America during the 1950s were told to finish their meals because children were starving in Armenia. Another saying that's been used to remind us of people whose lives are infinitely harder than our own is "I cried because I had no shoes until I saw a man with no feet." Over the ages, great verses, morality plays, and all sorts of other propaganda have pushed us into feeling grateful for what we have by keeping in mind the struggles that aren't our own.

This rule does have merit when it helps us experience gratitude and humility, as well as compassion for those whose lives include extreme struggle. The virtues of charity and grace aren't in question here. It's problematic because so often this rule is used to talk us down from the awareness of things that aren't right in our lives. It keeps us accepting injustices performed against us, both historically and in the present day. We're expected to accept social compacts that keep us "in our place" or on our side of the tracks, never crossing the lines someone else drew for us. "I'm good, I'm not starving or homeless," we tell ourselves as we limp along with a partner who does not fulfill our needs and has no interest in doing so, or with a bullying boss whose behavior we excuse as "a bad day." Forward we march, telling ourselves something about starving Armenian children, pretending that nothing's wrong, and reminding ourselves that we shouldn't question otherwise.

There's a hint of this problem in the rule's wording. Anytime we use the words "should" or "shouldn't," whether in your own headspace or out loud, it's a clue that we're trying to convince ourselves and each other to believe something we deep-down know is wrong. In this case, the rule is pushing past our legitimate pain. When we fail to acknowledge our pain, our struggle, our need for healing, the denial shows up in other areas of our lives. We eat our feelings, drink too much, spend too much time on the internet scrolling Facebook and Instagram. We become disconnected from our need to create joy and celebrate the uniqueness that comes with the particular *Homo sapiens* life we're living. We feel disconnected from our true selves and don't know why...or at least, we pretend we don't know why.

Rule 2: "You'd Better Tone It Down"

This rule teaches us to tone down and mask our independence, our creativity, our intelligence, our spunk, or any aspect of our being that somebody else deemed unacceptable. It is used to silence us and deflate our desire to be seen and known for who we are. It might even be used to threaten us when we voice injustices.

Over the years, many people have told me this rule. They were intimidated by a six-foot-one, transgender woman wearing heels in the Texas business world of the 1990s. What's more, I was smart, I knew how to look confident even when I wasn't, and I had a point of view. Still, I edited myself—which happens when we let other people's messes get into our heads. The words used by people who Other you to get you to behave in "normal" ways are clear and don't take much deep thinking to interpret: "Strident," "Bitchy," "Too flamboyant," "Too butch," "Too ethnic," "Too loud," "Too uppity." "You intimidate people." All convey that being "different" is our problem to correct or change. It's a veiled threat with a clear message: "You'd better get into the box I made for you and stay there. Or else."

How often have you heeded this rule to maintain relationships? Maybe you dumbed down your self-knowledge or pushed aside your own wants and needs so you wouldn't soar over an insecure partner. Perhaps you stymied a dream, a wish for a creative life that leverages your talents and gifts, in order to keep the status quo. We are fabulous peacocks, flamingoes, and birds of paradise who believe that we need to be pigeons, sparrows, and small brown wrens who shouldn't sing too loudly, lest we be heard. So we lie to ourselves and pretend we are happy being wrens. "Oh, I'm good. I didn't really want to do that anyway," we say as we talk ourselves out of pursuing our dreams.

The message to tone it down becomes so ingrained for so long that we ultimately convince ourselves that this "less than" life is what we truly want. The pressure to hide our Otherness works such a number on us that we become frightened of doing the bold and creative things we dream to do. So we sing a little wren song as best we can and pretend it makes us happy. In doing so, we starve our souls of truth, worth, and dignity.

Rule 3: "You Must Work Twice as Hard"

This rule says that if you're in any way different, you'll need to put in twice as much effort to arrive at the place where everyone else who is "normal" lands with ease. The tricky thing about this rule is that it has meant survival for many of us. It is a rule we learned to live by so we could work and function in a society that is not going to give us anything that resembles a fair shake otherwise.

Often, this rule is a legacy of power imbalances at the root of many, many of our stories as Other. Black people who were born in America know it well and can probably hear its words in the voices of parents, grandparents, aunts, and uncles. It's still real, and study after study of different aspects to Black professional life reveal how pervasive this is.

If you surmounted language and cultural barriers, not to mention hatred, in immigrating or making a life for yourself among a community of oppressors, you vividly understand this concept. Immigrant communities are still viewed with suspicion and contempt, and you may have been forced to prove your worth in a privileged nation that's perhaps benefited from the exploitation which caused you to immigrate in the first place.

If you've experienced sexual harassment, you also know well that a tremendous amount of energy goes into showing up as you keep yourself physically and emotionally shielded from aggression in the workplace and everyday life. You work twice as hard to deal with problems that many of your coworkers will never need to consider. People with learning disabilities, LGBTQ+ folks, and those whose Otherness stories came from the notion of being damaged or demented, all know just what this rule means because it has been our reality.

The shadow side of it places an unreasonable demand on our person. If you and I pranced over to the car dealership and each bought an identical car, but you drove yours twice as hard and fast as I did mine, whose car will last longer? Even after five years of driving this way, if you were lucky enough to still have your car in functioning shape, its condition would not be as good as mine.

People who spend their lives working twice as hard suffer inevitable consequences, including health problems, anxiety, and depression. The most insidious part is that even after working ourselves into poor health, we often keep at it. We aren't going to let anyone else determine that we're weak, lazy, or unable to handle stress...are we? Hell no! For some of us, this rule is so embedded in our beliefs that we refuse to pay attention to warning signs from our minds and bodies. Even as stress keeps us shedding pounds or packing them on, even as health warning signs flag us left and right, and even as mental health problems like anxiety and depression present with more and more symptoms...we ignore everything that tells us to slow down, rest, and take care of ourselves. Instead, we truck on by pretending the stress isn't there—until it hits us and we are flooded with the pain, tears, and rage of being so trapped.

Rule 4: "Oh, You Shouldn't Feel Resentful!"

This is a rule that operates in contrast to the first three, which tell us to accept our lots as less than others. While we're trying to exist under the crush of the first three rules, we become full of a resentment that we try not to feel. But we can't suppress the resentment all the time, can we? There are inevitably moments when we *do* feel it. In those moments, we acknowledge the injustices we experience as Others and become angry at the people who've inflicted the injustices upon us. This is fueled by the continuous acts of cruelty that we see all around us and that occur in our lives. If people in past generations of your family experienced severe oppression, your legitimate resentment likely runs deep. We yearn for those who oppress us to know the hurt they've caused.

If you're anything like me, you've fantasized a movie-like scene in which you strut into your high school reunion, head held high, stilettos clacking on the floor (work with me here). There you are in your most confidence-boosting and flattering clothes, perfect lighting, with a dazzling new haircut. Maybe we can throw in a wind machine while we're at it. All those mean girls and bullies stumble over themselves to apologize for their wrongdoings, perhaps finally sharing all these years later that they always admired you and were only mean because of their own insecurities.

Or maybe your guilt fantasy involves terrible exes who used your sense of Otherness against you. Maybe it's your parents, your siblings, or people at your family's house of worship who will tearfully admit they harmed you. They will realize that all the injustice you endured at their hands stemmed from their own inner turmoil and poor self-esteem, or perhaps simply their own misguided, unfair expectations.

A moment of truth: When we require someone else's guilt in order to move forward in our lives, we give away extraordinary amounts of our own power. Guilt from another person never truly allows us to move forward. Chances are, you know someone who's used guilt, age, illness, and isolation as tools to get what they want from others. This keeps those of us who've been Othered stuck in dysfunction, rather than able to deal with injustice and eventually move past it. These are dynamics that inevitably keep everyone miserable.

Of course, the abuse we and those we love suffer is infuriating. We hold onto the resentment and anger that sometimes seems white hot in intensity. But a fantasy of retribution is no more productive than a fantasy of guilt. Healing our soul from the pain of feeling cast as Other requires breaking the pattern caused by blind resentment. Remaining locked in a relationship dynamic that uses guilt as a weapon is a certain way to keep ourselves unhappy. Somehow, guilt is never satisfying. When we use it in relationships, we fan resentment among everyone involved. Whatever is gained from guilt we manipulate from another person is no gain at all.

Rule 5: "You Can't Change the World"

This is another rule that teaches us that the world is the way it is, and we can only deal with it. My mom used to tell me this one. The message was clear: the world (in our case, the suburban White one that was San Antonio, Texas in the 1980s) wasn't going to become a place that accepted gender nonconforming people. Nothing I could do was going to change their hatred, so I needed to accept the rules I lived under, as she did within the patriarchal and oppressive world that was hers. For me, this meant being a boy who conformed to the world as my family knew it.

I'm sure glad I didn't listen to her then. Today, she is too. Yet, her message is what we are all expected to believe about life. We're taught smallness and to think reasonably and practically in order to do well enough. The emphasis on conformity is strong. In fact, conformity is a cultural product we create and maintain as an expectation. This is because we recognize the pain that those who *don't* conform endure. So we talk about what we're "supposed" to do, with an outcome that we're told will give us a "good" life, which is free from pain and ostracism.

Still, we see the real-world terror happening in the here and now. Far from being based in irrational fears, we see the swastikas and hate graffiti at Jewish cemeteries and synagogues, reminding us that antisemitism didn't end with the Holocaust and that what happened to the six million can happen again. We see the shooting deaths of unarmed Black men like Ahmaud Arbery and are reminded that racism in America didn't end with Jim Crow. We see the stain of colonialism still bleeding through the four out of five American Indian and Alaska Native women who've experienced violence, the one out of two who've experienced sexual violence, and the numbers who go missing without an investigation (Indian Law Resource Center 2020). And we become so discouraged that we doubt our ability to change anything in a world of so much hate.

This belief in the world as a place where we have no impact and where despair is the norm is the most insidious of all the rules of fear. Instead of speaking out and refusing the status quo, we maintain it by staying slight, edited, scripted beings who do not claim our voices, our color, our spice, our dreams, our very existence. We go through life disconnected from our inner strength, our force. We refuse to speak up or show up for ourselves and others. The voice in our head becomes a motto we live by: "You can't have impact. You don't matter. Stop trying." So we stop being ourselves.

Understanding the Rules of Fear in Your Life

Rules of fear show up in our lives in different seasons, and while I suspect that all will ring true at some point, some rules may be more prominent in your life than others. You may find that working twice as hard is ever-present. Perhaps resentment and the tendency to neglect your needs when you're hurting only happen in certain situations. However the rules of fear affect you, we'll soon explore them in depth to help you identify the ways a particular rule shows up for your life and discover how to free yourself from its negative messages.

For now, know that the healing doesn't end here. You know in your heart that there's more to the process than accepting a deeply hurt version of yourself living under rules of fear. After all, you're reading a book by a transgender Texas woman who is a therapist and hangs out in New England sports bars with spunky octogenarian men in Red Sox caps. We can acknowledge that many of the rules somebody else wrote about life, social norms, and human worth were made to be broken.

What's more, we're living in a unique moment in history. Looking around, we can see that opportunities to be who and what we are have opened up across the world. This has happened because people like you and I are opening it. People from backgrounds and perspectives that span the globe, and the sexuality and gender continua, are bringing talents to government, arts and entertainment, higher education, the sciences, businesses. We are a big community of people who no longer need to exist in isolation. We see the growing pains and the resistance to this, of course. But this moment tells us we no longer have to abide by the rules of fear that resistance to change has placed upon our lives. Our spirit needs freedom to be and do so it can express as a voice in our consciousness.

CHAPTER 3

Gathering Tools for Your Journey to Freedom

Freedom. Just the thought of freedom from a job, relationship, or physical place that's making us unhappy is both thrilling and terrifying. This is because we dream to be free of things that don't work for our lives anymore, if they ever did, yet we feel glued in place by obligations and the assurance that while people, places, and things may make us miserable, they are at least familiar. We tell ourselves we stay for money, the kids, the security. "Better the devil you know than the devil you don't" is an old Irish proverb that warns us to choose certainty over the unknown. But the belief that life is a series of choices represented by one devil or the other isn't very nourishing.

We've often been shamed by our desire to have more and be more, so the idea of getting what we want seems out of touch and indulgent. You may even be in a state of hopelessness because you feel trapped in your current situation. Perhaps you've thought of freedom as something that other people do, but not you.

If your name was Pam, I'd say to you, "No ma'am, Pam!" because these notions of *can* and *cannot*, *should* and *should not*, are limitations that aren't at all helpful. A whole series of these types of statements have likely been with you a long time, and you may not realize it. The stories we tell about our lives and the way we construct notions of what we can and cannot do, who we can or cannot be, reflect a common theme: choicemaking.

Within us, we have the capacity to realize our freedom. There is a dreamer and a knower who can tell us what an authentic, genuine, whole life looks like. Yet there are also forces at work to hold us back, like obligation, shame, pressure, as well as real dangers from larger cultures and society. So we can survive in the world, the rules of fear have taught us to discount and disown that dreamer inside us.

Still, your desire for something different and better for yourself is there. It has probably been trying to get your attention for some time, perhaps showing up as the shadowy figure in your dreams, just out of direct sight. Maybe you see other people living a truth you yearn for and envy them for following it. Your envy is rooted in a desire for the very freedom you wish to express but are afraid of doing. Along the way, maybe you've learned to fear your dreamer, telling yourself things about devils you don't know. In many parts of our lives we become so risk-averse that we learn to stop dreaming.

Freedom doesn't mean that we abandon things that matter to us while following a flight of fancy. You don't have to change a single thing about how you're living right now if what you have works for you. You can stay at the same job, in the same house, with all of your relationships exactly as they are at this very moment. It makes sense if these fulfill you. Freedom is about choice and owning our right as the choicemaker, the architect for all we are, all we're doing right now. For the essence of freedom is to realize that we have agency.

These are pretty intense words, considering that for two chapters we've been ruminating on how Otherness has affected our lives. After all, it was someone else who cast us out, who beat us down to demoralize, humiliate, isolate us. It may seem a little unfair that we are responsible for our own healing when we weren't responsible for the ways we were wounded. Yet we are the ones living each of our lives, so it's you who has control over your life.

You are a decisionmaker who must determine, from this day, what you want your life to be. You have whatever situation you're in now. What shall you do with it so you are happier, more fulfilled, and clearer about your role as an architect of your life? Where can you find purpose and meaning? First, acknowledge that you were born with the capacity to choose. Choosing is the essence of freedom. You were born into, and continue to exist within, conditions that are specific to you. These may be grossly unjust…and yet, freedom is there, right now, for you to claim.

Even if for now you just want freedom from being labelled Other, so you can discover and embrace what it is you actually are, then this is enough.

For just a moment, close your eyes, take a nice deep belly breath, and notice how that word "freedom" feels. Allow it to conjure whatever images and sensations freedom brings to you: a sense of openness or vast expanse, perhaps the ocean or a grassy plain that extends past the horizon. It may also come as an unburdening of some sort, a movement away from someone or something that holds you back. The many images of freedom take us beyond limitations into possibilities, and bring awareness of how expansive we truly are. Just breathe this awareness in.

Now let's gather the tools you'll need for the journey into the great expanse of your dreams and choices, so you can experience the freedom that is your birthright.

Cultivating Clarity

Your clarity can address the complicated beliefs and mindchatter that come with the rapid information processing we all do. Clarifying the mental space occupied by a lot of rambling thoughts is much simpler than it might seem. I'm going to teach you an easy meditation practice to use as frequently as you wish. If you've never meditated, you may be surprised at how uncomplicated it is.

When you think about meditation practice, do mental pictures arise? Perhaps a row of Buddhist monks sitting in perfect stillness. The problem with an image of meditation like this is that it places the practice in the abstract, out of reach. This is like comparing ourselves to George Lucas or the designers on *Project Runway* in order to determine whether or not we're creative, or to Olympic athletes when we measure our body shape and fitness level. It's all-or-nothing thinking that keeps us stuck because it relies on faulty absolutes that make athletic ability, design sense, or the ability to meditate something we either have or don't have. Meditation is a means to break free of thinking in absolutes. Clarity is the result.

Every living thing on the planet breathes every day. Such a beautiful thing, the gift of breath, and unless we're experiencing respiratory problems, we breathe without noticing it. Instead we get caught up in the whirlwind of our thoughts, to-do lists, finances, or relationship problems. I *should* go study. I *should* call her. I *should* dust that nasty ceiling fan. Mindful breathing allows us to clear this tendency, freeing ourselves from its destructive hold. Slow and conscious awareness of our breath is the simplest thing we can do to free ourselves.

If you're dealing with significant trauma, breathwork may not be the best mindfulness practice to start with. You can instead choose to focus on a neutral part of your body, like your hands, and proceed to work with your thoughts as follows. You might focus on a neutral thing in your environment, like a bookshelf or houseplant, that you can contemplate and experience nonjudgmentally. Either way, do what feels right to you.

CLARITY MEDITATION

Get comfortable in your chair or wherever you're sitting. Read these instructions or go to http://www.newharbinger.com/46479 to listen to a guided audio recording. Then, for about a minute, either close your eyes or cast them down slightly to allow your gaze to gently fix on an object or the floor. If your eyes shift out of focus while doing this, just go with it.

Breathe in through your nose, if you're able to. Take in a deep breath that fills your lungs and that makes your belly swell. Then, release it more slowly through your mouth, at about half the speed of your inhale. Remember to keep your eyes closed or resting on your object.

If you have an interrupting thought about something you should be doing, like "Am I doing this right?" or "The lawn is growing while I just sit here not mowing," notice it. Label it *thinking,* and let it float away. Try not to count the passing seconds either, as this will be just another mental distraction.

Just notice the breath as you inhale and as you exhale. Do this for about a minute, longer if you wish.

As you return to reading this, notice the things you experienced with the practice. You may have struggled with interrupting thoughts and even gotten a little judgy with yourself. I get it. Meditation feels foreign the first time we do it because we hold a lot of shoulds. Whenever this happens, just return to your breath or whatever your object of focus is. Free yourself from judgment and carry this practice with you to do as you need it while working with the material in this book, and beyond as you work with life.

You may have begun encountering stuff, even during your short meditation, that's sitting below the surface, such as unacknowledged emotions, physical pain, or a yearning for self-care that you don't often give yourself. Perhaps you had a combination of experiences: seconds of calmness and attention to the present moment, followed by a lot of distracting thoughts and beliefs, the realization that you were thinking, and a return to your breath. It's all part of the practice.

The emphasis on breathing as a method for freeing the mind is one of the first instructions in many meditation practices, and it's how I start my therapy groups. Learning to notice the flow of breath is one of the most transformative things we can do for stress and anxiety. By stilling the mind and noticing the moment, we transform it. The tangled knot of distracting thoughts that's almost constantly with us is untangled, the threads of mindchatter momentarily blown away by the breezes.

As you go about life events for the rest of today, tomorrow, and throughout the week, notice the moment. Before you hit "Send," head into a meeting, make a phone call, or start the car, take three deep belly breaths. Follow the inhales and exhales with the same level of attention you just brought to your brief meditation. These breaths will instantly slow you down in the moment and bring you back to a stillness that's free of anxious thoughts. Practicing this more frequently can significantly reduce the stress you have in daily life. Your mind will be clearer, increasing your ability to see colors, hear sounds, and feel textures in a way that you haven't before. This sets you up to behave in ways that are less dictated by external stressors and intrusive mindchatter. This is what happens when we take in our world through a clear mind.

The way you move into any moment, and move out of it, demonstrates the power of choice you have. You have the ability to shift into awareness of how each moment is shaping your reality. The way you attach to events that stress you by engaging your Otherness story may feel automatic, but if you slow down your thoughts, there is a point of decision. You can decide to attach to stressful events and old patterns of behavior that were conditioned by the rules of fear, letting them drive you. Or you may make the decision that both the event and your attachment to it reflect choices to hold on to stress—choices that you don't need to make. To acknowledge this is a powerful step on the journey to freedom.

Having Self-Compassion

As you begin learning the practice of cultivating clarity, it helps to recognize not only the distracting thoughts that you have in the moment, but the places where old mindchatter thoughts have taken you in the past. Clarity also involves looking at your past with clear eyes. The ability to look back on the life choices we've made with *compassion* is necessary for the deep journey work of healing the damage from living under old rules of fear. Crystal's story helps illustrate this.

> *Crystal's story of Otherness was rooted in her experiences of childhood poverty that persisted until adulthood. Raised by a single mother who suffered from depression, from a young age Crystal had to dress herself and help care for her mother's needs. Crystal's peers at school bullied her for the second-hand clothes she wore, calling her mother a "crack head." As she got older, Crystal was desperate for friends and was willing to do whatever it took to gain people's approval. She even became a bully herself, sometimes stealing money and belongings from smaller children. Starved for affection and approval as she moved into adolescence, her desire for approval led her into sexually promiscuous behavior. She struggled to say "No" when someone was offering affection. Ultimately, these encounters left her feeling hurt and exploited.*
>
> *As she began mindfulness work as an adult, she began healing from approval-seeking tendencies. Nonetheless, the shame from her adolescent behaviors of bullying and sexual promiscuity remained with her. Whenever memories of her teenage years surfaced, she felt disgusted and angry.*

Like Crystal, we carry shame for past behaviors. We regret actions we took, even thoughts we had and emotions we felt. We regret things we did in our youth and stuff we said or did yesterday. We've done things for love, money, or validation. There were things done in desperation that we wish hadn't happened. Sometimes we just did things because we didn't know any better. We've broken hearts, betrayed secrets, gossiped. We've made decisions in positions of power—perhaps as parents, partners, supervisors, or simply as individuals who had some degree of unearned privilege—that we now know were harmful, making people's lives harder in some way. It's all there. Our humanness.

We are more than our shame. Shame is only a reaction to beliefs we have about ourselves in the world, the things we do, the methods we use for encountering and tackling issues—and those beliefs are often false. As you look back over the story of your life, there's a decision to be made. You can remain locked in shame, regretting all the things you did and didn't do. I really hope you won't. It helps no one to weigh yourself down with mistakes you've made. Of course you see things you wish you had done differently, after you did them. This is the process of learning, and it's what gives retrospect such value.

The choice I hope you'll make instead is to honor those times, even the hardest ones. Don't glamorize the road not taken. You didn't take it at the time—and that's in fact what led you to this moment. It awakened your need to heal, to become mindful, to accept your past and move forward into the future of your choice. In learning to do so, you're gaining the tools for transforming the rules of fear that Otherness instilled.

Acceptance of the past and gratitude for a healing present are what's here now. If you and I took a stroll through the years of your struggle together, I suspect we'd find someone with a lot of mindchatter, many burdensome external messages, and a lot of hurt. We'd see that this person was trying to cope and find purpose—and to deal with something that wasn't their fault. Finding compassion for the hard times of the past is a foundation for learning to exist in a healthy present. Here is a tool for finding this compassion.

HOLD YOUR PAST COMPASSIONATELY

Prepare for journaling by grabbing a pen and some paper or your favorite notetaking device. You may want a notebook or file, as many activities in this book call for journaling. Begin the process of locating the part of you that really needs compassion right now by doing the Clarity Meditation. If you have a different meditation practice you prefer, by all means, use it now. Then read these instructions or go to http://www.newharbinger.com/46479 to listen to an audio recording that will guide you through this practice. Then begin writing.

After bringing yourself into the present moment with your breath, allow your memory to scan the chapters of your life. Perhaps there's been a shame story calling for your attention as you read. Using your breath as a tool to anchor you in the present moment, allow your memory to skim your past until you find the shame event that deserves your work right now and reasonably tests your strength. As the event comes to you, situate yourself, and follow these steps.

1. Notice the setting and the people involved. Where were you? Who was there?

2. Witness yourself at that age and season of your life. Only, instead of seeing yourself through the eyes of who you were back then, at whatever age, see that person in the scene as if you were watching a movie on the big screen.

3. Notice how your younger self was navigating the world. What was that younger version of you seeking in the world that you really needed? A physical survival need like food and shelter? An emotional need like love and acceptance? Maybe it was some other need that you couldn't articulate at the time. See if you can put words to what the character you see on the screen needed.

4. Allow this scene to widen in scope so you can see the world that this younger version of you was navigating. Notice the forces working against the character, both in the physical setting and in close relationships. What were the scariest and most threatening elements of the movie? What was the larger social context that may have held the character in states like fear and desperation?

5. As you watch this younger you trying to find what was needed, what do you feel for the person? Notice what arises as this character attempts to navigate the world, and that situation in particular, with the life skills and beliefs that you had at the time. Just let the observations wash over you.

6. Write down a title for this movie and a description of what you discovered about yourself by seeing through this lens.

It's humbling to recognize ourselves from an outsider perspective, as a character in a movie, for we can see how our younger self navigated a complicated world with limited tools. We perceive the context and the desperation borne of necessity. We may even begin to feel protective toward our younger selves, similarly to how we feel for the character who's desperately trying to survive in a favorite movie.

Awakening to the odds stacked against us, and how we struggled to survive, is the heart of self-compassion. Witnessing ourselves as scrappy survivors, who stumbled through life making the decisions that circumstances seemed to call for, makes it more difficult to feel ashamed for the choices we made. We can compassionately understand what happened.

Of course, we may also notice that righteous anger emerges upon witnessing the ludicrous life predicaments we've had to deal with. Anger precedes acceptance, so I invite you to recognize the necessity of anger as you compassionately witness your story of Otherness in your life journey. Then, as you grieve the fact that you had to struggle as you did, you can recognize the responsibility you have to yourself in the future. Doing this draws on the tool of creativity.

Applying Creativity

Most of us who are old enough to remember Gladys Knight and the Pips understand the song "I've Got to Use My Imagination" as an account of moving on after a major relationship loss. The ability to move forward from adversity, whether a troubling relationship or any other devastation in life, requires us to imagine a future that's better than present circumstances. That ability to imagine comes from creativity—a key to overcoming adversity in life.

If you consider yourself a creative person, great! Or maybe you don't, and as you see the creative genius of others, you use their light to diminish your own. These beliefs about ourselves are rooted in childhood messages, like much of the source material in our lives. I acknowledge that the weird little leaf thing I made in fourth grade for the Fall Festival wasn't all that, but when my teacher laughed at it, she didn't inspire my artistic talents. I came to believe I lacked creativity, despite the probability that her judgment was due to "creating" something by following very specific rules and directions, rather than tapping into actual creativity.

I realize now that the ways I made do, found resources, and pulled together a series of life choices were in fact extremely creative. Your ability to find your way and make do is at the heart of creativity too.

Creativity is a capacity we all have. Creating change for our lives begins in the same way that writing a book, baking baklava, or weaving a Gullah sweetgrass basket begins. We put our imagination to task. We bring together notions of what can be, whether it is thoughts to the keyboard, honey to the puff pastry, or love, tradition, and nimble fingers to the basket weave. It all begins by imagining the possibility of what's to come. The alchemy of this exercise is that we're creating our future.

CREATE YOUR PATH

It may be helpful to once again begin with a simple one-minute Clarity Meditation, and to add three steps.

1. As you follow the breath and arrive in the present moment, feel the work you've already done releasing the current stressors of the moment, the false beliefs that say "I can't," and the shame that kept you locked in the past.

2. Release these as you exhale. Allow the parts that no longer serve you to wash away.

3. Then, holding yourself in the present moment, look straight ahead and experience the horizon. Because you've committed to no

longer allowing Otherness to feed the belief that you are unworthy, sense the promise of freedom ahead.

When you're ready, prepare to write a short story. It can consist of a few simple sentences or a few pages. You will write down what your future self will be doing. Then you'll write about how your future self will be feeling and thinking as a result. To keep "I can't" and "I shouldn't" from rearing their heads to block you, write the narrative in third person, using your name and pronouns. Apply the definite language of a plan that's already coming into place. Something like this:

> *Janessa is moving home to Georgia next year. She'll be back with her sisters and so many people of her chosen family in the place she adores most. She'll once again go to art lectures at the High Museum and take her nieces to lunch and the zoo. She'll have picnics and dinner parties to go to once again, and head to the beach at Tybee Island in summer. She's going to experience looking around at faces she loves, feeling contentment and gratitude for being home.*

You get the drift. Now write your future.

Through this method, the story of your vision can be told. Once something has been given voice, it's out there as part of your reality and you can give it space, force, and energy. Describing yourself in the third person can evoke new sensations. In the experience of writing this vision, a number of things can happen. Do you...

- notice how right it feels and realize it offers a truth you know you need to fulfill?

- judge what you wrote?

- feel shame for giving space to your dreams?

- encounter cynicism about whether you can achieve them?

- want to move toward the vision you've written down, yet you worry about how the decision will impact others?

- feel overwhelmed by the practical implications and all the pieces to the puzzle?

You're likely to feel some mixture of these. As you consider your response to the exercise, you can see the specific parts of yourself that feel locked in place, even as you envision the future you want for yourself. You may encounter a lot of "Yes, but..." and "Not now" statements, as well as many "What if...?" questions about obstacles that might arise. I get it. Forging ahead toward a dream is daunting in the moments before the first step.

Yet when the dreamer chooses, so many powerful things are put into motion. After discovering the creativity to envision a future that reflects what you truly want and need for your life, the next task involves taking practical steps toward the dream. You have the power to bring this future to fruition. You can do so with sass.

Acting with Sass

Sass is the bold, resilient, spirited essence of our nature that yearns to be free and take the necessary steps to act on our dreams. It's the determination, spunk, and spice needed to move forward. This tool will allow you to trust yourself during the journey toward the vision you created in the last exercise.

Creativity is the way we imagine possibilities and sass is the fiery spirit we need to live them. It takes audacity to live a dream, as it feels hard to break rules that have governed our lives for so long so we can do the thing that is right for us. This is something that relatively few people are willing to do. This is a good time to tell you the story of my friend Sassy.

Sassy St. James was a transgender drag entertainer who'd already been living in her female role for more than a decade by the time we met in the late 1980s. The culture in San Antonio, Texas violently oppressed the LGBTQ community when Sassy was growing up and coming out. Her experiences of life in poverty and not conforming to the rules for Mexican American boys of her era added to her struggle. Nonetheless, she chose to live her truth as a woman. As a beautiful, talented, backtalking comic of the drag scene, Sassy was the life of the party. She chose the name for her stage persona to claim a space within the world, to represent her need to be seen. She experienced violence, hatred, and a number of personal dangers over her lifetime. Yet she persevered. As Sylvia, which was her chosen name for when she wasn't on stage, she had a rich life. Surrounded by her family of choice, she was loved and continues to be honored even decades after she passed. If Sassy could make a space for herself in the world, you can too.

Review the story you wrote in the Create Your Path section of this chapter. This version of your future may look radically different from what you're doing now. But chances are, when you think about it, you can see some actionable steps required to get there. Some things, like getting a college degree, saving money for a move, taking a lifetime trip, or rearranging professional or domestic situations, may take a long time. So looking that far into the future seems daunting. But the years will pass, either way. The choice about what you'll do during these years is yours.

Sass is about choosing to take those steps toward your vision with audacity. A "sassy mouth" talks back. You need to backtalk to your mind-chatter and tell it that you in fact *do* have what it takes to live the life you want. You *can* march to your own beat. Or you can prance. It's your life to create. How do you want to act?

SASSING BACK AT "I DON'T DESERVE THIS"

Review the story you wrote in the third person about your vision for yourself that reflects a yearning for change. Once again, first gather your focus through the Clarity Meditation. Then get your journal or laptop to respond to these questions.

1. What's one thing you can do right now to move toward your vision? Write this as an affirmative statement: "Right now, I can..."

2. Notice what the experience of that action is, as if you're already doing it. Really feel the energy of your forward motion. What does it feel like to be taking this step?

3. Consider what will help maintain focus on your dream. When old patterns that tend to lock you in place set in, how can you return to the vision behind what you're doing? Be specific about the old stuff that might come up, as well as the actions you'll take when that happens.

4. What strengths do you expect to develop along the way?

5. What talking back must you do when the old mindchatter tries to tell you that you don't really deserve your choice?

Sass feels pretty good, doesn't it? You're owning your power to choose, so remember to practice clearing the muck that comes up along the way. Because it will. Mindchatter that says, "I can't" and "I shouldn't" shows up. Everyone who moves into boldness and confidence, every person who moves forward with a vision, has to learn to roll with life experiences that present along the way.

My mother often says that a master gardener is someone who's killed at least a thousand plants in the process of learning to garden. This is exactly what happens when daring to live with a dream and purpose. Everyone who's left a terrible life circumstance had to adjust to something new. Striking into the new and unknown is going to be messy. Speaking up to someone who has held you down is daunting, and it doesn't always go the way you plan. Going to college will bring disappointing grades at times. New relationships don't always go easily or work out as wished. New cities turn out to be more expensive, hotter, colder, or noisier than we'd like. The place in the country we fantasized about is buggy and remote. Writers create non sequiturs that don't make sense in the first draft.

All of those things happen because someone took a risk, one they had to take to discover the possibility that lies on the other side. Our ideas don't always pan out as we hoped, due to lots of circumstances. Yet we keep at it. We realize that ultimately there's no devil in the unknown. Rather, the unknown offers new opportunity, new chances. When we trust ourselves to love, to learn, to show up in these important life situations, we can create a whole new series of possibilities that are truer to our nature. We learn to live free and get better at it for the very reason that we tried. To accept our creativity, however it exists within us, is to know that the path may involve some slips, slides, and missteps. We continue anyway—with clarity, self-compassion, and sass.

Bringing the Tools Together

Each of our tools—clarity in the present, self-compassion for the past, creativity for designing our future, and the sass to act so it can happen—has a distinct role in our overall mission. They free us from the muck of shame we were forced into when we were cast out as Other. As you become accustomed to new ways of thinking and doing, they become more habitual than the old, shame-based ways. What's fed grows and what's starved will die.

Perhaps it's time for you to allow shame to die. In its place a stronger and more confident version of yourself—the one you've manifested in this chapter through your efforts—will emerge. Let's draw on that version of you to face the rules of fear that have governed your life until now.

PART 2

BREAK THE RULES OF FEAR BY REFUSING TO STAY STUCK

CHAPTER 4

"You Shouldn't Complain, Because Others Are Worse Off Than You"

This rule of fear reveals how we survive by denying the hurts that are there. We accompany it with something along the lines of, "Chin up, don't let things bother you so much. The past is the past." We try to live by this, telling ourselves that we should have gratitude for all the terrible things that aren't befalling us in this moment. After all, if we've got roofs over our heads and food on our tables, there's no reason to ever be unhappy. We should dry up those tears and move along with life!

This mostly works, except for the times we struggle to find gratitude because we're haunted by sadness and a sense of futility that we can't quite shake. Then there's the lifelong struggle with crushingly low self-esteem, convinced as we are that we're not actually worth much. Add all the moments of feeling like an imposter or a phony in our careers, which bleeds into doubting our worth as partners, in our families, as friends. We feel like damaged goods so much of the time, which alternates with feeling ashamed because we believe we shouldn't feel this way. Old wounds reopen whenever we interact with people who seem to know just how to demoralize us a bit more.

We've worked hard and are brave. We've learned to shield vulnerability by trying to maintain an exterior that doesn't match what we feel in our hearts. This has been necessary for survival. Showing weakness to people who cast us out as Other, revealing that they've hurt us deeply, isn't something we can do. We have to show the world that we're unbothered, laughing off pain or working harder to be "bigger than that"—bigger than the people who Other us. As big and courageous as we are in the face of everything from microaggressions to verbal or physical assaults, what happens in the moments when we're absolutely depleted from having

to always be the bigger one, the bolder one? Dolores's story may help you
see how this works.

*As a Latina growing up in a de facto segregated neighborhood of
Denver, and the older sibling of a brother with spastic cerebral palsy,
Dolores had to develop skills for dealing with Otherness from an early
age. There were many Othering experiences: the condescension and
cold White stares on the other side of the town's invisible racial
border, implying "You don't belong." Defending her little brother from
school bullies who mocked his gait and body spasms. Dealing with
being laughed at and taunted for the thick glasses she wore until she
was fourteen.*

*Quick-witted and brave, Dolores learned how to use logic and a
fair dose of humor to parlay the insults and cruelty of a racist and
ableist world. After witnessing her brother struggle with physical
bullying and neighborhood children facing tough challenges, Dolores
came to believe that "Others have it harder than me." As a result, she
defended others and became the kid always seen at the lunch table
with the most rejected and isolated of peers.*

*Her skills in addressing mistreatment would be put to the test
throughout her teenage and young adult life. Dolores helped her
mother manage the progressive responsibilities of her aging
grandparents and her brother in a system of healthcare disparity for
Latinos. Upon beginning a career in the aviation industry, she
experienced numerous incidents of sexual harassment. When she
found out how common this was among female coworkers, Dolores
became a union steward and leader so she could advocate against
mistreatment for herself and others.*

*As courageous and unflinching as she needed to be for everyone
else, conditions hurt Dolores deeply. Her brother continued to endure
cruelty, her grandparents were dismissed callously by healthcare
workers, and she was never, ever able to live through a day without
feeling that she and the people she loved were Other. She felt the strain
of near-constant vigilance, grief, and exhaustion. Deep down, she*

*doubted whether she was truly strong enough to be everyone's
protector.*

When we look at Dolores's story, it's not hard to see deep psychological wounds that Otherness has inflicted throughout many parts of her life. In order to care for herself and her family, she's devoted significant amounts of energy to being an advocate fighting for equal treatment. As a union leader, it was her responsibility to always appear strong, competent, and poised while championing the rights of her colleagues. But whatever power and social capital she had didn't extend beyond the workplace.

Consider the deeper, internal struggles that Dolores dealt with. She was degraded for her heritage and gender, core parts of her identity that have been treated as Other again and again. There's complexity to letting her vulnerability be seen. She had to protect parts of herself, for her own psychological wellness and that of her family.

Protection and self-preservation often mean cutting ourselves off from our hurts, denying that pain exists. *Yet the pain does still exist.*

Shame is such a strong force in our lives that we feel vulnerable whenever we're not able to pull ourselves up by the bootstraps and deal with deep wounding on our own. We've valued composure to such a degree that we've learned to bottle our own pain and never talk about problems, for fear of coming across as weak, whiney, or vulnerable. We tell ourselves that we should "get over" or "get past" things, then blame ourselves when we're haunted by them.

You no longer need to convince yourself of anything. Othering has left deep psychological and emotional wounds that you must see and acknowledge in order to heal. Now you have tools for that healing.

We must first address the shame you feel about voicing pain and stop treating your Otherness as trivial. It's true that other people have it bad, they may have it worse than you, but that doesn't obviate your own pain. You don't have to pretend that gaping emotional wounds aren't there. Through voicing untold stories from your life and recognizing unclaimed places in your body where you still carry hurt, you can begin to heal.

To truly heal our pain, we must first name it. By naming the burden we've carried, we create the opportunity to finally lay it down. As we become more skilled at this, we create a pathway for recognizing things about ourselves that are joyous, fierce, beautiful. With that in mind, let's explore a little more about where you picked up this rule that "You shouldn't complain because others are worse off than you."

How You Learned to Bottle Up Emotional Pain

Many of us were taught to deny or suppress pain from an early age. Crying is a natural response to both physical and emotional pain, yet we feel self-conscious and even ashamed about our tears. It's easy to see where we get such ideas. "I'll give you something to cry about," is something many crying children were told by parents who probably received similar messages themselves. The implication was that tears are unacceptable and so are weakness and vulnerability. For a child, this translates to something along the lines of "I am unacceptable when I cry," "The things that cause me pain *shouldn't* cause me pain," "It's not okay to admit weakness."

Growing up, this message was reinforced each time we were teased, shamed, and humiliated for crying or otherwise indicating pain and weakness. We need to cry in response to the problems in our lives, to physiologically express the pain of social exclusion and Otherness. But we can't. This may still be true for you today.

You may have learned to suppress tears and sadness through expressing emotions that are considered safer. One "safe" substitution is based on the gender norms we were raised with. "Boys don't cry." But the misogynistic cultures many of us were raised in say boys can become angry, they can bully, they can assert power and become aggressive. They can treat girls and women like objects and trophies. They can use intimidation to rise to the top…of whatever or whomever they were trying to top. Those who don't do these things are often ridiculed as weak or effeminate.

Most girls were not taught to name their needs in a clear way. Being a "nice girl" means hiding feelings, wants, and insecurities under a veneer of social rules that follow the order of what her culture says a woman's place is. Many learned ways to hint at what is needed and then wait for others to catch the hint.

So many people of all genders pride themselves on not showing or naming pain. The belief runs deep that vulnerability equals weakness, which opens the inevitable pathway to having our insecurities exploited. The truth is, sometimes it can happen that way. But trying to kid ourselves by denying our pain won't prevent us from experiencing it. In fact, denial makes things worse.

When Pain Is Not Acknowledged

Unnamed hurts don't simply go away because they're inconvenient. We've become skilled at trying to push away unpleasant thoughts that are associated with memories we'd rather forget. The result of all this work to suppress emotions does a lot more harm than good. Emotional suppression has been found to increase stress (Webb, Miles, and Sheeran 2012). It decreases self-control as well as the ability to think clearly and problem-solve (Richards and Gross 1999). Long-term, people who suppress emotions tend to experience greater incidence of anxiety and depression (Kashdan, Elhai, and Breen 2008; Low et al. 2017), have more difficulty pursuing personal goals, and struggle to communicate their goals with romantic partners (Low et al. 2017).

As much as we may have valued our ability to disconnect from sadness, jealousy, fear, anger, and other uncomfortable emotions, we do so at the expense of our mental health. This is because when we suppress emotions, they don't simply disappear. The memories that incited them stay with us, and the sadness, regret, and anger we have about them linger as well.

Our inability to express our range of emotions can be so severe that we instead carry them as a series of body pains and illnesses. In a real sense, we swallow our pain. What we've swallowed shows up as gastric problems, muscle aches and tensions, and stress headaches—to name a few conditions. We can cause additional problems when, in our efforts to deal with stress, emotional suppression leads us to be extremely hard on our bodies.

When we use emotional suppression, it becomes difficult for others to feel close to us. If you've ever had someone deflect a sincere compliment, you understand what I mean here. Or perhaps you're one who doesn't take compliments. When this happens, the person doing the deflecting is keeping the person giving the compliment at a distance. Continuously distancing people who wish they could express love, gratitude, and feelings of high positive regard for us will lead to one inevitable outcome: loneliness. This is because when we do not allow the warm, squishy feelings that come with accepting gratitude, we make ourselves emotionally inaccessible. If you do not allow yourself to be accessed, people will eventually stop trying.

> When Dolores's brother passed away at forty, she felt the loss deeply. Nonetheless, she also felt obligated to stay strong for his wife and two daughters as well as her parents and grandmother. She struggled to grieve openly and was quick to deflect efforts made by extended family, friends, and coworkers who tried to comfort her. "Go see my mom," she'd tell them, always conscious of the pain others were experiencing but struggling to acknowledge her own. When friends offered assistance and invited her places, she turned them down for fear of becoming vulnerable if someone spoke about her brother. As a result, people stopped inviting her, leaving Dolores more isolated yet unable to name how painful isolation felt.

Like Dolores, we can struggle with asking for help when we need it or accepting it when offered. So often, it's easier to show up for others' needs and support them to deflect needs of our own. We're pretty lousy about collapsing into the supportive arms of those around us. Yet, if we don't let people know what we need or how to respond to us when we hurt, they're certainly not going to guess. Those supportive arms won't be there if the people they're attached to don't feel needed.

Much of this struggle with asking for help and accepting it, and discomfort at the prospect of relying on others, is rooted in a strong reaction we have to feeling pitied. Let's explore this more closely.

The Intense Aversion to Pity

Being pitied feels terrible. For an article in *Family Circle* magazine titled "What Are You Looking At?" (Reicherzer 2016), I interviewed mothers from across America whose children had a conspicuous difference, such as autism, a visible scar, or any characteristics that people in public stared at or judged. While the mothers' experiences varied based on the unique needs of each child, there was a resounding chorus about feeling aversion to people's displays of pity. Whether it was sad glances from strangers before averting their eyes or assumptions by close friends and family that a mother needed comforting because of her child's experience, the moms were adamant that pity was unwanted. In fact, it was seen as condescending. Of all the things they needed—for someone to engage their child, a night off from the demands of parenting, or more accessible schools to meet their child's needs—they did not need pity. This aversion to pity that the moms felt is understandable, for when people pity us, they are casting us as Other.

When we sense people's pity, it feels a lot like contempt, doesn't it? It doesn't come across as empathy, but as a superiority over this "pitiable" part of our life—whatever that is. When we have an adult crisis, we can keep it secret for this very reason. Anyone who's gone through a divorce understands that part of the difficulty isn't just the traumatic grief of dissolving a marriage and relationship. It's also the social shame and humiliation we feel facing the world, believing that others pity us for our inability to keep our marriage.

Therefore, things we believe will invite pity, like divorce or a health problem, aren't often discussed. We keep our chin up, even if we have people in our lives who'd listen, accept, and respond to us with loving kindness. We don't reach out because we don't know how to be vulnerable without fearing that our weakness will be pitied. We tell ourselves that *others have it worse* and pretend that things aren't bothering us, even as our emotional lives fall apart.

If you've spent your life dealing with people who use pity as one more way to Other you, perhaps you constantly try to prove all the ways you're neither weak nor deficient. Yet there's something within your emotional reaction that deserves attention, if you'll allow it. Your emotions are there to tell you something about your need.

Emotions Can Be Your Guiding Light

A wonderful therapist friend of mine used to say that emotions are a barometer. They're neither good nor bad, even ones we don't like experiencing, such as jealousy. They arise to help us regulate our world. When we feel joy in response to a certain kind of music or food, or with a special person, we want more of it. Why? Because joy is pleasant! When we're frustrated by the never-ending highway project, we stop driving through it and find another route. Why? Because frustration is unpleasant. Jealousy tells us there are things we want but don't have, while disgust tells us exactly what repels us.

The more we are aware of the various emotional responses we have, we can more clearly choose paths that lead to joy. If joy is a guiding light, then we can choose to surround ourselves with joyful things. If we don't acknowledge when things make us resentful, sad, or jealous, we'll continue to create the same situations that lead to these feelings.

We have a full range of emotions that help us see and respond to things like abuse and injustice. When I worked with family violence survivors, they often shared how the abuse wasn't so bad, that things could be much worse. "He only slapped me. He didn't really hit me that hard. It could be worse." When it got worse, they ignored that too.

Feelings can offer great promise. When we admit to ourselves that the red flags we see in life, through painful emotions that offer warning signs, are telling us something—then we can choose. You can truly learn to trust your instincts, responding to that small part of you that says, "No, I don't quite think this is right." To begin learning to connect with this truth of yours, this part within you who knows there's something better, let's do some excavating by building on the Clarity Meditation exercise you learned in chapter 3.

Gaining Clarity About Your Pain

You've been pretending your pain doesn't exist for some time and likely wonder what can happen if you were to instead register the pain you've felt. Just the prospect of acknowledging pain can sound overwhelming and scary. I get how scary it feels. After all, this is a rule of fear that has allowed us to use other people's pain and struggles as a method for denying our own.

Fear is transitory and will pass. As you've seen from the previous exercises, you have tremendous agency in which parts of your life you choose to address at a particular time. To further support you, I'll teach you some grounding exercises that you can use if you get overwhelmed by feelings.

I'm also going to offer you a couple of different ways to experience mindfulness. Yes, you can use stillness and the meditation steps from chapter 3 to free yourself from distracting thoughts. It can relieve the "shoulds" and "musts" that perpetuate negative self-talk. But this isn't the only path to mindfulness. Music and dance free body and mind, allowing rhythms and beats to disrupt our usual mindchatter. Mindfulness is a form of paying attention that you can apply to any number of experiences: your breath, music you love, movement of your body through dance, and any kind of calming or creative activity.

I tend to use a fusion of methods, as there are moments when I need to honor my right to be still and experience the majesty of a given moment. Other times, I need to free my body and mind of inhibition by allowing music to move me into rapture. You may find music or dance especially helpful if you've experienced body shame and are self-conscious about the space you take up in the world. Here is a meditative method to attain a more active state of mindfulness and clarity based in mindful movement and dance. The method you use to reach this clarity is up to you.

EXPLORE THE RIGHT TO BE SEEN AND HAVE NEEDS

Get comfortable in your chair. Read these instructions or go to http://www. newharbinger.com/46479 to listen to an audio recording of them. Then, for about a minute, either close your eyes or cast them down slightly to allow your gaze to rest on an object or the floor. If your eyes shift out of focus while doing this, just go with it.

Breathe in through your nose, if you're able. Take in a deep breath that fills your lungs and makes your belly swell. Release it through your mouth at about half the speed of your inhale. Remember to keep your eyes closed or fixed on your object.

If you have interrupting thoughts about things you should be doing, such as "Am I doing this right?" or a to-do list arises, notice it. Label it "thinking" and let it float away. Try not to count seconds, as this will just add another mental distraction.

Just notice the breath as you breathe in and as you breathe out.

As you continue your breathing, notice the part of your journey that's needs attention now. As you read about inhibiting pain, you probably thought about parts of your story that you struggle to accept. What is it that needs to be given space now?

You've used the rule "You shouldn't complain because others are worse off than you" to silence your story. Chances are, something deserves to be grieved: an old hurt, a part of your life that isn't what you want it to be, a yearning that has not yet been fulfilled. Don't label this thing with a lot of unnecessary, judgmental terms. Simply allow it to emerge, perhaps as tears, a sound, a name, or however else it surfaces. Whatever form it takes will be exactly what's needed at this moment.

As this experience of yours, this part of you, expresses itself, simply be with it. Don't shame yourself for feeling what you feel. It's a part of your story that you're honoring by bringing it into the now. Welcome it into your awareness, for its existence in your life as a past hurt or present worry is getting your attention for an express purpose.

Notice this part of you, however you've coped with it over the years. What you're now experiencing is part of a grief or injury. While it once haunted you, what you once feared is an area you now can see.

Practicing clarity in stillness is especially helpful to deeply listen to your body and your spirit. As was true for Dolores, there's often a message just beneath the surface from a part of ourselves yearning to speak its exhaustion, resentment, or grief.

For Dolores, the clarity exercise brought her into contact with the profound grief of losing her younger brother, who had been her best friend. She felt anger at the lifelong mistreatment he received in response to his spasms. Guilt arose because she felt that she hadn't done enough. She began acknowledging anger and sadness over how her family had been treated throughout his life, and memories surfaced of her mother's constant worry for both her children's safety.

An ongoing breathwork practice can help you silence the daily mind-chatter that accompanies your life. It allows you to move deeper into spaces of healing that acknowledge pain and also clarify the parts of your experience that bring you contentment, excitement, and forward momentum.

Some of us find a lot of solace in music, with particular genres evoking different moods. Music that's very soothing, such as New Age or spa music, can be useful to accompany the stillness exercises. We can also carry a lot of emotional inhibition, so I encourage you to find a way to embrace movement that works for your body. Dance is a central component to healing work in so many cultures because it releases us from the need to control things. We can release emotion through music and experience spatial freedom when we allow our bodies to move. Dance therapy is a powerful form of healing.

EXPRESS FREEDOM THROUGH DANCE MOVEMENT

Begin by finding a musical genre that invites you to move freely. I suggest instrumental music because listening to vocals tends to focus our attention on lyrics. For this exercise, your body is providing its own lyrics. Jazz has wonderful freestyle forms, and there are Latin styles that blend with jazz—like salsa, samba, and bossa nova—to encourage movement. Perhaps you find strong African drumbeats freeing or feel drawn to electronica, trance music, house music, or fabulous disco. Search through a streaming service until you find the music that speaks to your yearning for freedom and makes you feel alive. Then create a space where you can tend to your own needs, away from those of others.

Be free. Allow music to move through your body so movements occur as a spontaneous flow of experiences. If you feel self-conscious, just notice this, allowing your body to continue its movement and find the freedom it's yearning to express. Allow the parts of you that have yearned for freedom, and can no longer accept suppression, to move. Locate the part of your body that has carried your sorrow about Otherness and invite it to move. Just be with movement and the power that comes with reclaiming your absolute right to be in the world. The whole purpose is the movement itself as you come to accept your body without shame and your right to take up space.

Chances are, whatever emerges for you during these exercises is something you've kept hidden for a reason. Perhaps it was too hard to look at. Maybe you were trying to protect yourself from pity, or it seems too deep a sorrow, anger, or hurt to handle. As you uncover this part of your own story and see it for what it is, it's yours to accept without judgment.

Whatever your truth is, it doesn't need to haunt you. You don't need to hide things from a fear of pity or because they seem too overwhelming. The work you've done has prepared you for this level of introspection, and you're now more aware of your strengths. The next step is to choose what to do with the information about yourself that's emerging.

FIND THE COMPASSION TO ACT WITH COURAGE

Grab a pen and paper, your keyboard, or whatever else you may be using to journal. Then I invite you to choose a mindfulness exercise and engage it to arrive in a state of personal clarity so you can answer the following questions.

- As you've allowed this part of you to emerge in whatever form it has taken, what have you learned about yourself?

- What's a major part of your story that still needs to be grieved?

- Within this experience of discovery is also an opportunity to acknowledge the strength it takes to do this kind of deep work. What's it like to trust yourself to go this deeply into introspection?

I'm big on self-praise when we start getting into this level of work, so offer it to yourself. It's courageous to start looking closely at the parts of ourselves we've neglected and to begin doing these deep fixes. That's what you're doing here. You're addressing the parts of yourself that keep you from living fully.

This is a great place to bring in your creativity. With creative thinking, consider the part of yourself that you now feel more aware of than you did before. What attention does it need? Is there an action that needs to be taken? Or is this simply a part of your story that needs to be honored?

As Dolores began acknowledging more of the Otherness grief she'd held for her brother, herself, and the rest of her family, she recognized how exhausted she felt. Her exhaustion came from years of trying to be "the strong one" for everybody. As she moved deeper into self-understanding, she acknowledged that she wanted to be seen for her hurt and have a space where she wasn't always "on" for someone else.

UNLEASH CREATIVITY BY INTENTIONALLY HONORING BLESSINGS

Close your eyes and observe the part of your story that emerged when you did the Exercise to Explore the Right to Be Seen and Have Needs. See the tremendous courage it took to get as far as you have. Feel your fierceness and know that you have strength within you, whenever you need it. You don't need to deny your pain, your truth, any longer by comparing it to other people.

Notice the strengths and resources in your life and write them down. These can be big or small. They can be within you or outside of you, whether things others did for you, things you did for yourself, or things you didn't do at all but are grateful for. There are no expectations here.

Then ask what you need to do right now to honor these forces in your life. Your response can be another introspective activity, like an intentional and loving ceremony in your garden to commemorate yourself, that you create for you. Or it can be a shared, social exercise. If connection is what you need to honor what's in your life, create an outing with people you love or perhaps make a series of phone calls if they are far away.

You can also honor the healing opportunity you're giving yourself by voicing your desires. Honor new language by describing ways you're learning to become aware of the fear, shame, and Otherness that sat within you all these years. When you find people who can listen, there is power in knowing that so many people are healing along with you.

Whatever you choose to do to honor the positive forces in your life, it is an expression of your freedom. It's a gesture of noticing all the things you have within you that can act in the service of your wholeness and your freedom. From there, you can dive even deeper into this capacity to act by using your sass to talk back to the voices of shame that have limited you all this time, forcing you to silence your true nature and your own pain.

Sass is a powerful tool for addressing this rule of fear in our lives. Even as we grow by doing this work, we easily slip back into old patterns of thinking and behaving. When we do, our old shame voice takes over, telling us we failed at being able to heal. Shame tries to show up in many ways. When we fail to voice our truth about an important matter, say "yes" when we mean "no" and don't keep an important boundary, or return to any wounded ways that existed before our journey of freedom began, we sink into shame. We need our sass in these moments because sass can tell shame to shut up and go sit down.

CLAIM SASS AND TALK BACK TO SHAME

You can talk back to your shame voice when it attempts to speak up. It's pretty simple to do, actually. The role of sass is to demonstrate to the consistent illogic of shame. Here's how it works.

Choose an area of your life that tends to take you back to shame. Listen closely to get a sense of the shame voice that arises. Whose voice is it? Maybe you continue to shame yourself in the voice of your grandmother or brother or boss, and identifying its familiar tone will reveal a lot. Also notice the types of messages this voice sends you.

Then imagine your sass voice coming from the most confident part of yourself. You know you've got it in you. Get fierce, baby! That's the part I want you to feel.

Write out a dialog in which you start with a common shame statement that you tend to tell yourself: "You're too fat," "Nobody's ever going to love you," "You're too stupid," or whatever else there is. Reply to each shame statement from your place of confidence, with your sass, and question it or point out things that test the shame's validity. Here is a sample dialog.

Shame voice: Just be glad that someone wants you at all. You should stop being bothered by your marriage.

Sass: Why is it irrational to be bothered that he's checked out all the time?

Shame voice: Well, your folks managed to stay together in spite of their problems.

Sass: They were unhappy too. Dad drank and stayed out late. Mom pouted until he bent to her will. A lifetime of misery isn't better just because it's familiar.

Shame voice: Well, you're not smart enough to venture into the unknown and look how fat you've gotten. You'll spend your life alone!

Sass: Maybe I would be a single for a time or forever. And maybe it would be scary and lonely at times. But I can date, have friends, and do things I want to do. Some of the loneliest times of my life have been in this marriage, so I really don't have anything to lose.

Shame voice: You'll be alone and stay alone. Nobody will like you!

Sass: It's a big world with a lot of people doing many things. Who exactly is nobody?

As you keep at it, you'll find that shame will eventually wear down. This is because it's impossible for shame to hold up to logic. In the example, it's clear that shame is a voice that uses extreme language like "at all" and "nobody." The statements aren't verifiable and lack evidence. The validity of shame's opening statement, "Just be glad that someone wants you at all," can never be established. Try your own dialogue and talk back to shame, questioning each of its premises until you've debunked the false logic. Make this a regular practice whenever shame tries to suck you back in.

As you become more skilled in this, you'll find that your shame voice's power and influence decrease significantly. When it does show up, you'll recognize it for what it is and have the tools to address it.

Muting our story of pain and the right we have to name it has been a theme to this point. We didn't want to feel our hurt, and most certainly didn't want others feeling pity for what they perceived our hurts to be. By freeing ourselves from the false belief that our pain is trivial, we strengthen our ability to move forward with life. As the tendency to suppress emotions and pretend our concerns aren't real loosens its hold, we grow in self-knowledge and the ability to articulate our needs.

What's more, we stop being bound by worrying about other people's pity because, just as we grow in our ability to experience a fuller range of emotion, we become able to correct those who try using pity to Other us. We also learn to recognize others' compassion when it is genuine and accept it. "No, I don't require pity," we might say. "But I do reserve the right to have my beliefs, my feelings, and my needs acknowledged." By approaching the relationship from an undiminished place that indicates, "I am as deserving as you," we create the opportunity for real change as we claim the space we're in.

CHAPTER 5

"You'd Better Tone It Down"

The next rule of fear we encounter as we deepen our introspection has origins that may be simple to trace if people used these actual words to correct our behavior. By seeking to correct you, they were implying a clear message. Something about you, your being, your personality, your physical presence, your hair, your swag, your swish or your race, culture, gender, sexuality—and how you expressed these—was incorrect.

As you repeatedly heard this message, you may have come to believe something that sounds an awful lot like "I am incorrect. I am not good enough as I am. There is a right way to behave, and I can't fit that mold being the way I am. I have to change, to become somebody else." Carrying such a message through life perpetuates a lot of hurt because you try to be what you are not.

Perhaps you doubt yourself and feel a need to control aspects of your character. You may feel self-conscious and socially anxious in a variety of situations in which you are conspicuously different. This mix of doubt and fear keeps you from showing up as you'd wish, as you. Instead you cut things away: trying to change the way you speak or look, hiding relationships from people you fear will judge them, refusing to share opinions about things that matter to you. All this cycles back into shame when you get mad at yourself about opportunities lost along the way.

Despite whatever or whomever provided the source material for "You'd better tone it down" and may even now be using this rule of fear to colonize your spirit in an effort to control you, it's time to heal the erroneous belief that you're incorrect and not good enough.

So you can understand how and where to use the tools of change for your life, we'll first explore the types of messages that are communicated under this particular rule of fear. Doing so will allow you to clarify the sense of incorrectness that keeps you most stuck and in pain.

Understanding Messages of Incorrectness

The messages we're given that tell us we're incorrect often focus on aspects of our being that people in positions of unearned privilege believe we shouldn't have or do. We've been told we're too loud when we're happy or excited, too talkative when we have ideas to share. We're too flamboyant, too in-your-face, too strident, too bitchy. We're too provocative, too flirty, or maybe too reserved. These move into attacks on how we go about meeting basic needs for ourselves. We're too needy when we require love, affection, attention; too cold or distant or even dramatic when we need time to ourselves; too interested in an activity or subject that isn't what people like us are supposed to care about; too much showboating or acting arrogant when we're proud of things we've done and want to feel celebrated for them. Never mind that what we've accomplished is possible because of what we've overcome.

The messages also target qualities innate to our physical or mental being. We're "too smart for our own good" or the wrong size, skin tone, or gender for what we're wearing or how we're behaving. Maybe we're too direct, too mouthy, too intimidating when we express legitimate grievances to people who prefer to keep directness, mouthyness, and the right to intimidate reserved for themselves. Laverne's story helps us see this.

> Growing up in the rural South, Laverne knew well that "You'd better tone it down" actually meant "Conform to our expectations of who you should be and what you should do, or else…." She knew that "or else" could lead to lynching Black males and bombing Black churches whenever White racists felt the need to reassert power. After 9/11, she saw business owners who were Muslims and Sikhs (mistaken for Muslims) threatened until they closed up shop and moved away. And when her gay uncle was outed in a local media shaming scandal during the 1980s, she witnessed his humiliation.
>
> Within this setting, Laverne had to work extremely hard to disguise the fact that she was a lesbian. She feigned interest in boys and pretended to have innocent crushes on male celebrities of the day. When she was fifteen, her father caught her kissing a girl, and Laverne found out what it meant to be gay in her family. She was

forced to undergo a year of conversion therapy to shame her into becoming heterosexual. This effort included a summer camp that applied fundamentalist Christian religious themes to change Laverne's sexual orientation.

In the years that followed, Laverne toned down any aspects of appearance and behavior that might suggest she was a lesbian. She kept her head down and was unwilling to even befriend another girl as she tried to appear focused on school and maintaining her family's social compact with their church community. She smiled and pretended to be grateful to the couple who ran the conversion camp. Meanwhile, she suffered from flashbacks of her time there and nightmares about her "therapist." When she was alone, she cried— feeling isolated and trapped, wishing for death while fearing the hellfire she'd been told awaited her. She spent the remainder of her adolescence trying to play her role in a complicated social compact of silence and conformity, ever fearful of the "or else" threat.

You too may have felt required to uphold a social compact that meets the needs of an oppressive culture. By toning down aspects of *You*, so others weren't uncomfortable with your existence, you may have avoided placing yourself and people you love in danger. The following list will help you recognize this rule of fear in your own history. In your journal, record all the ways you've been told or forced to tone down, silence, or modify yourself in order to meet someone else's needs.

- My physical presence or some aspect of my body

- My expression of sexuality

- My expressions of love

- My gender expression

- My pride in my race or culture

- My spirituality or nonbelief

- My mental abilities

- My appearance and how I present myself

- My hobbies and interests

- My physical abilities

- My voice

- My emotional needs for love, affection, and respect in relationships

- My need to verbalize issues and opinions

- My creativity

- My beliefs about what is just

- My human rights

- My right to choose for myself

As you read through these messages and reflected on parts that are true for you, you may be noticing that "You'd better tone it down" has come from more than one source. Perhaps you heard this from parents and extended family, teachers and peers at school, or elders in your religious or cultural community.

In some cases, the message was delivered because authority figures feared harm might come to you, whether through violence or emotional abuse. Like Laverne's family, they may have feared for your spiritual well-being. Later in the chapter we'll explore the role Otherness may have played in their lives. Whether or not Otherness was a factor in their behavior, or they had some kind of justification for their actions, the emphasis in this book is your need to heal—here and now. This rule of fear is part of your story and the trauma you experienced is legitimate.

Your voice and your ways may have also been silenced by people—even a vast population in society—who have no interest in protecting you from harm. Their intention is to preserve their own well-being and power, and your voice and presence was—and perhaps still is—seen as a threat. Let's dive deeper into the role of oppression as a tool that's used to silence us.

The Role of Intentional Shame and Demoralization

When the intent is to demoralize and oppress, this rule of fear is best understood as part of a societal dictate that includes a threat. "You'd better tone it down, know your place, accept your role, and don't expect anything more than we'll give—*or else* the punishment will be severe. Stay on your side of the tracks and you'll be okay." What your side of the tracks actually looks like varies for different people, but it might be something like "Marry a nice boy [or girl]" and "Have the number of children we tell you to have." It might include "Work the job that suits your station" and "Live in this area designated for folks like you"—however that's defined. They'll proceed to tell you how much money you "deserve" to make and what attempting to live outside your station, area, or expectations for you must cost, financially, physically, emotionally. In other words, the dominant group that's defining these rules says, "Know your place," and act in service to our rules.

Just reading these messages can bring up fear, as they imply that forms of violence are the primary tools for enforcing your role in society. We know what *or else* means for us, just as Laverne did. The direct threat of what's to come if we don't maintain our place—whether through our home, our family, our community, and our roles within all these—teaches us to keep major parts of our lives under wraps. The fear that's instilled remains with us into adulthood, as Laverne's story shows.

> *Laverne graduated from college and moved to a large city where she forged a close circle of friends who were both LGBTQ and allies. But she continued to face the daily decision that causes many queer people to struggle: how and when to come out. Because she worked as an elementary school teacher in a state where people can be terminated for sexual orientation, Laverne feared backlash from parents who didn't want their child taught by a lesbian. Coming out would have caused disruption at the school and in her personal life.*
>
> *Now in her mid-fifties and married to her female partner of fifteen years, Laverne experiences an ongoing dilemma when her*

students' parents, upon seeing her wedding ring, ask about her husband. She has dodged these questions by creating a story about a husband who works overseas for most of the year. Keeping her marriage hidden is Laverne's way of maintaining safety for herself and her wife, financially, emotionally, and physically.

Whatever messages you've received, the essential force behind them tells you to stay in your lane and not act up, call attention to yourself, or do anything you aren't supposed to do. You've carried whatever society dictated as expectations for being "well-behaved." This rule of fear essentially says that if you stray from what you've been taught about people like you, you are in danger of rejection, ostracization, job termination, violence, even murder. Break the rules and the rules will break you, because rules are made and changed by people with the power, money, and guns to enforce them.

Whether the people who demanded that you tone yourself down did so with hostility or a belief that they were protecting you, the result is pain and deep loss. You've likely spent so much of your life dealing with a sense of being incorrect and out of step.

The Sense of Being Incorrect

At the heart of this rule of fear is neverending self-consciousness. We are haunted by a feeling that we don't belong. There's valid evidence for feeling this way in our own story and the stories of people like us. Our daily words and actions feel contrived as we walk a tightrope so we don't slip up and invite danger. We often feel like poor actors who are faking it to meet social expectations for who we're supposed to be.

Our self-consciousness doesn't end once we get out of social situations. In our heads, we get stuck in repetitive thoughts that beat us up for things we said or did, and how we might be perceived as a result. We obsess about events that occurred in the past and about how we'll perform in the future. We rehearse toned-down scripts of who we think we're supposed to be, spending a lot of time on safety planning just to navigate life. We move through life feeling controlled by the role we're trying to play.

This lands us in a distressed emotional state in which we are always on high alert. It's easy to see how this occurs for us. In chapter 2, I shared how experiences of rejection during childhood lead us to expect rejection later on. Now, because we're fully aware of differences that were sources of feeling Othered earlier in—and perhaps throughout—our lives, we walk into society and relive our experience of feeling Other in the present day.

In this heightened experience of rejection sensitivity, we go through life not trusting a world that has taught us all too often that it cannot be trusted, that we are not safe. It's important to emphasize that in a power-imbalanced world, our safety may be tenuous. Using personal history as our guide, we continue to go into experiences feeling guarded, waiting for bad things to happen, and anticipating rejection.

This is how a rule of fear operates in our lives: In addition to legitimate fear that being different from a dominant culture can lead to, we become so focused on the tightrope of living and navigating in a confined, toned-down role that we lose ourselves in the process. All this fear, and the places it takes us, diminish our quality of life. We feel depleted from having to reference our lives to their lives and defeated that we have no choice.

Being cast out as Other has a significant silencing effect on us. As I've discussed, it silences our voice by limiting us to a narrow role for people of say, our gender or race or sexual identity or more. The more insidious effect is that being Othered inhibits our ability to listen to ourselves, ask ourselves what we deep-down need, and then respond. We're so busy acting and reacting to the experience of Otherness in our reality that we constrict the parts of ourselves that could be quite robust. With that in mind, let's apply our tools to the task of retrieving this lost voice of yours that deserves to be heard.

Gain Clarity by Visualizing the Parts You've Toned Down

To begin recovering the parts of yourself that have been lost, recognize what you've toned down. It's time to examine the dreams and promises you've shelved and uncover new ones along the way. The process of gaining this clarity begins with meditative work. Please feel free to use stillness or dance or another practice, as you wish. The important thing is that you clear your mind of distracting thoughts so you can be here now, fully present. I suggest reading through the entire set of instructions before starting this practice. Or you can go to http://www.newharbinger.com/46479 to listen to a guided audio recording.

· As you move from your meditation into this clearing process, bring to mind that place where it seems you buried various dreams, needs, ways of thinking, and styles of existing in the world. Spend some time getting a mental picture of what's been buried for too long. Peer into it. Illuminate the parts that you cast away and now need reclaiming.

Allow this buried part of you to come into focus. See it, hear it, touch it. This essential piece to your puzzle has been waiting for some time. Is there…

- a life goal that needs your attention?

- a need to finish something you started long ago and have put off for some reason?

- an identity, a love, a part of your story that you need to claim for yourself and perhaps proclaim to others?

As you bring this part of you into focus and see what is illuminated from the depths of silence, allow what's surrounding it to also come into view. Are there related parts of your experience that were cast away alongside this dream? What's the bigger story that is now asking for your attention?

As you start to clarify the parts of yourself that are yearning to breathe, to be given life again, to be awakened and actualized, you may recognize that a lot of things suddenly make sense. Through lightbulb moments of "Ohhh! That's what this is," we even see the hints that have been arising throughout our lives to try moving us toward freedom from whatever was trapping us.

This is also the moment when all the distorted beliefs you have about yourself, and perhaps about the people who've helped enforce those beliefs, may push back to reassert their influence on your life. If you find that reasons you shouldn't do or be something are bubbling up, return to the breath or to dance. Doing so will bring you back into clarity and a state of awareness. This is extremely helpful when racing thoughts—the internalized voices of those who've Othered you—start telling you to tone it down again.

As you continue these exercises, it's important to go easy on yourself. If all you have time for is three deep, intentional breaths, do that. To moving toward freedom from racing thoughts that keep you in a heightened state of rejection sensitivity, you must free yourself from the harsh self-criticism you've used in the past. To help you make this shift, we'll use compassion and creativity together.

Compassionately Recognizing the Ancestral Struggle

Compassionately understanding our life circumstances is so necessary for self-examination and life change. Our understanding can't be self-punishing. Sometimes we look back at situations from the past and ask ourselves, "What was I thinking? What was I doing?!" and proceed to beat ourselves up. It's so easy to get mad at ourselves for loving the wrong person, for making the wrong investment or career choice, for placing our family's and society's expectations of us over our own wants and needs. We beat ourselves up for all the things we said and didn't say, for all the lost opportunities, and for whatever we gave up as a result of this rule of fear.

Now that you've recognized what's been lost in the morass of Otherness, you can acknowledge the truth that your experiences as Other placed you in circumstances that take a long time to recover from. Whatever beliefs became instilled along the way and whatever you learned as methods for coping with these circumstances, these were the tools you had at the time.

These tools were handed down from people in societies, past and present. They were often handed down to us by our families too. Part of healing from Otherness, with compassion, is looking at how the rule "You'd better tone it down" also influenced the lives of your ancestors, those in your family tree and lineage. How did the culture in which your family lived shape the way that they responded to you? As we explore this question, remember that no part of this discussion excuses Othering behavior. But it does help you put that behavior in context, understand it, and figure out how to heal it.

When you consider what you know of your family tree, it may not be hard to recognize that legitimate fear existed for your ancestors. These fears that foremothers and forefathers had for the safety of their children made their way to you. Perhaps you can even perceive the role that caution and anxiety played in the guidance you received to tone down behaviors or qualities your family believed would get you into trouble.

As you go deeper into this family history, perhaps you can see people who were Othered in the same way you're Othered. While extraordinarily hopeful that those of your generation would enjoy a better life than their own, perhaps these people were also deeply afraid that this would not happen.

Trace your roots back to cataclysms that befell your people—however you choose to define "your people." Consider the role of violent oppression in their lives, people who were Other like you, and the multiple oppressions experienced over centuries and millennia as tribes of humans colonized, enslaved, and brutalized each other. Down the timeline of history, the means for survival in societies that were very broken were passed down. Otherness isn't new. Even twentieth-century events shaped our families and the communities in which we were raised to form an understanding of how we are supposed to look and behave.

UNLEASH CREATIVITY BY HONORING OUR ANCESTORS

Grab some paper and a pen. Returning to a meditative state, allow your mind to drift back over what you know of your historical timeline. Whether you're able to trace your lineage back for generations or know very little about your birth parents and their ancestors, this exercise can be modified to fit your needs. If you know little about people in your biological family, or if your ancestral line is partially or entirely unknown to you, for this activity you can claim an ancestor who symbolizes an early version of your struggle. For this exercise, you are invited to draw from what you know.

Reflect on the experiences of an ancestor, real or chosen, who lived through a particularly difficult personal challenge. Perhaps they were one person in a whole culture that suffered through a tumultuous or cataclysmic period prior to the 1950s. If you lack specific historical data or points of reference, use what you know of your race, culture, and the lives and experiences of people like you. This chosen ancestor can be anyone with whom you feel an aspect of kinship.

In writing, explore the life challenges this ancestor endured that were a central narrative for any period of turmoil. What was this person's biggest survival struggle? Follow this narrative, letting your writing flow in any direction it takes you.

Imagine this ancestor looking into the eyes of their children or people who came next in your lineage. What would the ancestor wish to be different for them? If you chose an ancestor with a shared sense of community and kinship, contemplate what this person likely wished could be different for subsequent generations of people like themselves.

If the ancestor were to consider all the struggles that they endured, what would they wish for you to be doing now? Write a short narrative of this ancestor looking toward the future and imagining your freedom, which they could not have. Only write this narrative in first person, as if you could see through their eyes: *My name is Isaac and I work on a fishing boat....* If you can write in the language and vernacular of the ancestor, this may help bring you even closer to the experience. Or if you're inclined, draw a picture to symbolize their worldview and dreams for your freedom. Give yourself enough time to really feel the effect.

My hope is that this exercise helps you experience every healing choice you make now as a way to honor your ancestor's struggle. Someone, somewhere dreamed that you would be free. They probably wouldn't have understood what "freedom" means in today's context. But their struggle for the freedom of future generations, to give you the ability to make your own choices and live without shame and fear, is precisely what you're bringing to fruition right now. In turn, you can hold such a dream for your decedents and future lineage.

Compassionately understanding how more recent generations adapted to survive, and endured trauma stories, is your next step on the healing journey. Let's explore that now.

CREATIVELY HONOR MORE RECENT FAMILY HISTORY

The last exercise brought you to explore an ancestor's story of yearning for your freedom from hardship when the ancestor could not experience it. With this in mind, bring to mind the home of a parent, grandparent, or great-grandparent who was a child-rearing adult between 1950 and now. Then work through these prompts in your journal.

What were the struggles, fears, worries this person had for themselves and the children of the house? What was this person's Otherness, as you understand it? Was there an aspect of their identity or their self that they were Othered for, or were they representing whatever was "normal" in their historical moment?

What was the "rock" in their lives—the thing this person depended on completely? It could be religion, the community, nature, a spouse, alcohol. Identify whatever served as the person's anchor and foundation when things were rough.

How did this person's life reflect the hopes and dreams of their ancestors?

What rules for being did this person transmit to their children in the form of musts shoulds?

Write or draw a first-person account of this person's story, as you did in the last exercise. This time really emphasize the struggles and choices they had to make.

As you explore the stories of both your distant ancestors and more recent lineage, you can begin to recognize patterns in place that molded your childhood and set the expectations for you as an adult. By doing so, it becomes possible to resolve conflicts that exist within your family when their values differ from, and have at times stifled, your own. You will recognize patterns within the culture you grew up in, surrounded by people whose familial circumstances—at least in terms of norms and values—were probably similar to our own. Or perhaps you grew up in a cultural borderland surrounded by people whose backgrounds were different, and you can recognize patterns in the dynamics of engaging neighboring cultures. Notions of race, religion, gender roles, and social class were shaping life then and continue to do so today.

At times, it can feel easy to resent parents and people of their generation for the decisions they made when rearing us if those choices underscored our own Otherness. However, it's also important to recognize that their thinking and ways of engaging the world happened in response to the world they occupied. We tend to judge the past, particularly when it comes to our own families and communities, through the prism of what we know now and how we now see the world. In doing so, we fail to honor their struggles—no matter how well or horribly they seemed to function—as a strategy of survival for them and for our lineage.

Again, I'm not excusing abusive parents and family systems. What I'm offering is a way to recognize the experiences that shaped people who Othered us and to situate those experiences in a larger, stratified system of time, place, and Otherness. By encouraging this view, I hope to help you begin resolving the stuff they burdened you with. Yes, they may have played a role that instilled this rule of fear, but they may have also struggled with the oppressive force of this rule their whole lives without healing. Unlike them, you now have new tools, like clarity, compassion, and creativity, to reclaim the parts of you that have been lost.

> As Laverne made this discovery, she had to acknowledge feelings of deep betrayal and outrage over her father's decision to place her in conversion therapy, her mother's assent, and the continuing humiliation of being forced to attend a church that supported this abuse.
>
> When she reflected on her own parents' histories, Laverne began to see deeper into the social compact they'd made to create and maintain a social order. This compact, forged in the religious convictions and social ties of the Deep South, was how her parents'

communities had survived uncertainty, struggle, poverty, and grief. Coming together in faith and social solidarity with neighbors and people in their church community had endured for generations.

Laverne saw that this legacy social environment had damaged her life, and led to the eventual decision to leave her hometown and break ties with her parents. Healing began when she could name her abuse. She concluded that "They do not deserve forgiveness for betraying me and I'm not offering it. But I release myself from the shame they used in their own lives and from the lies they believed about God. That was their shame, their beliefs, not mine. I am divine in my spirit. They are not allowed to haunt me anymore. I'm glad that I'm here and I'm past this. I know that I can never accept the abuse I endured being inflicted on any child."

Like Laverne, we must also honor our own survival decisions, relative to our ancestors, that we choose irrespective of who they were and how they existed. With these tools, you can reclaim your space in the world, own your right to equality, and promote freedom in your life and in your expressions of need. Honoring your lineage and the systems that existed for you, and the people you know and love, brings you the ability to discern what to take with you and what to leave behind. Let's use the tool of creativity now.

HOLD YOUR SELF AND YOUR STORY WITH ACCEPTANCE

In this exercise, we'll combine our creativity and our compassion to help heal the piece of us we toned down and tried to efface. Healing comes through the practice of *acceptance*. Bring to mind the part of yourself identified in the exercise Gain Clarity by Visualizing the Parts You've Toned Down. Hold this *You* close to your heart as a gift and consider the following. You can also listen to an audio recording of this exercise at http://www.newharbinger.com/46479.

1. Feel any frustration toward the previous generation or other parts of your family or culture, who survived according to the rules of their time.

2. Recognize their struggle and, if possible, accept who they were and the choices they made. This is a powerful way to free yourself from these things.

3. Bring to mind the family members you resent the most. Allow yourself to feel their struggle, and yours—not as a child being knuckled under their own angst and fear. Instead, be a witness to the continuing story of Otherness.

4. Visualize your parents, their parents, and generations of people before them forming progressively larger circles around you. See through the fears, the desperation, even the bitterness, abuse, and jealousy. Then witness your own freedom as a light arising in the very center of the circles. Hold it close to you.

Freedom is a powerful gift for our own spirit and for people who've been denied freedom of their own. It's the answer to the yearnings and promises that so many people had no idea how to fulfill. Now you're gaining tools for finding your freedom, embracing it, and living it as a truth that can guide you.

We looked into the depths of the silence we were forced into when we were told we'd better tone it down, and we witnessed all that is there. By shining a light on it and identifying the very structure of our fear, what holds it together, we saw how our hopes and dreams and ways of being came to exist as whispers. We saw the yearnings our ancestors had for our freedom. And we witnessed legacies of trauma and Otherness coming down through the ages, through our parents and grandparents as they experienced their own stressors and even atrocities.

Identifying the parts of ourselves that were silenced brings us to a logical conclusion: we now have a choice to make. We make the choice to live free of this rule of fear and no longer let it keep us pretending we are things that we are not. It's time to embrace ourselves as choicemakers, free from the message to "tone it down" because we are able to decide what we want our lives to look like and pursue that vision.

CLAIM SASS SO YOU CAN LEARN TO LIVE BOLDLY

Grab your journal. Once again, bring to mind the part of yourself that you want to reclaim from silence. Taking a few deep belly breaths, move into an aware state. Then write down answers to the following questions.

- How will you express this part of you in your life now?

- What's the ultimate payoff for living your truth, your vision, your dream?

- How does this payoff radiate to benefit those you care most about, even if they won't see effects immediately?

- What part of you is saying this vision is right for your life?

- When people and systems try to pull you back toward old, out-moded roles that work only to serve them, how will you remind yourself of this commitment to live freely?

Your answers to these questions will tell you how to move forward with whatever it is that you've now reclaimed.

As Laverne worked to bring sass into her life, she recognized that she and her wife needed to more intentionally seek spaces where they can live out as a lesbian couple. While Laverne acknowledged that being out at the school where she worked still presented too great a risk, the couple determined to build a stronger local network of queer women friends. They made plans to spend a summer vacation at a queer-friendly destination, and even began talking about eventually retiring to a community that is LGBTQ centered.

Breaking this rule of fear is all about embracing the parts of your life that have been silenced in the past and refusing to accept oppressive limitations in the present. We don't require that someone else define what's appropriate for our role in life, our place. We don't need to be told what's ladylike, what's queer, what's too much, what's pretty, what's acerbic or strident or bitchy or uppity or obnoxious or funky. Words like "you'd better," "you should," "you can't" is language used by people and systems who seek to control our ways of being. Being sassy takes back the naming rights for our lives.

It's time to stop giving control to others and begin claiming your rights, your spaces, your light. You don't owe apologies for how you represent yourself. And that "edit" someone wants to make to your character or the choices you make? No thanks. The critics can keep that for themselves. Sass is about freedom from domestication. It's about living a truth that's real even when nobody else sees it. You don't need permission anymore.

As we go about the task of reclaiming our rights to voice, expression, creativity, and all the other components lost to us through toning down, it's a valuable pause point. We now see the parts of ourselves that are genuine, strong, spicy, lovely, fierce, and hidden for so long. Hidden, that is, but not lost.

Our yearning for freedom is a force that's much stronger than shame. Through this yearning, we're on the path of reclaiming ourselves. You are not Other, as you no longer need to be frightened by, or anxious about, the parts of yourself that you previously toned down. Whenever these old feelings arise, remember to breathe. Embracing the colors, the textures, the sensations of *You* is what this chapter of your life is all about.

Know that your retrieval is still beginning. Whenever you're in doubt, always come back to your breath. As you start the practice of showing up and bringing your full presence into the room, new experiences will emerge. You'll uncover other parts of yourself and discover experiences that your toned-down state would never have allowed. Whenever you locate more parts that need to be retrieved, notice these so you can return to this chapter when you're ready to reclaim them.

CHAPTER 6

"You Must Work Twice as Hard"

If your life has felt like an uphill climb, it's not a stretch to visualize this rule of fear as an extraordinarily tall mountain with a summit above the clouds. Yet this mountaintop isn't a destination you want to reach. It has been belching sulfur and stinking up your life for as long as you can remember.

In a society where power is extremely imbalanced and unequal, we face a significant challenge: we constantly have to prove our worth. Beyond our childhood trauma, ongoing Otherness experiences insist we must prove ourselves to a culture, family, workplace, or community that is consistently seeking to disprove us. Weak and inferior, crooked and greedy, lazy and untrustworthy, sex-crazed and unstable, dumb and exotic, weird and moody—whatever the dominant scripts are, these are samples of the labels we're constantly working against. We each know these scripts so very well.

Many of us try to prove ourselves by rescuing people around us. We're the bankers, mediators, middle-of-the-night movers. Often, living by the "you must work twice as hard" rule keeps us locked into endless commitments as fixers of the broken, rescuers of the weak, champions of the diminished, sages to all who seek our wisdom and patience. If you find yourself being someone people count on for all things, chances are the favor has not often been returned. By following this sense of obligation, we wipe ourselves out. All the while we pretend we're fine. We insist we're not running on reserves, lest we appear less than strong and unable to tackle whatever problems life, and the people in it, throw at us.

This rule of fear also makes our goal-setting run amok. The message that we're Other tells us our worth isn't guaranteed. We need to prove it, and keep proving it, by finding ways to make up for our difference and perceived inadequacy. So we set goals and orient toward the future. We work so hard to reach goals, we miss the sights and textures of the present moment. Once we reach that goal, we're on to the next, and then the next. We keep making the uphill climb throughout our lives, often realizing—once it's too late—all we missed along the way. Let's examine what this rule of fear has meant to you and how it may show up in your life.

The Many Ways We Work Twice as Hard

This struggle may include working more than one job and balancing life on a shoestring budget. You may work twice as hard because life offers you little choice if you're going to feed yourself and your family. For people who have faced bullying and discrimination, who've been rejected, exoticized, treated as "less than," and otherwise cast out as Other, working twice as hard has many additional meanings. You may do it to…

- prove you're worthy of equal rights, equal pay, and equal access in a society that has denied you these things.

- prove that people like you aren't lazy, incompetent, immoral, or unstable.

- find someone who will love you exactly as you are, including your mind, body, and history.

- obtain your family's approval, acknowledgment, or what you think their "love" is.

- prove something to yourself, even though you're uncertain exactly what that is.

Just as people who've been physically starved of food spend the rest of their lives terrified it will be taken away, when we've been love-starved, approval-starved, or emotionally starved, we work desperately hard to obtain approval and feel like we matter. Nina's story illustrates this.

Nina was born into a family with unstated gender roles that were fairly simple. Boys and men had exalted status. Girls and women were there to support them. The youngest of four children, Nina's homelife was spent assisting her mother with chores and politely listening as her mother vexed about the trouble Nina's brothers were getting into, the cost of her sister's cheerleading uniform, how hard Nina's father worked, and other concerns of the day. Although Nina was a good student and performed particularly well in science and math, her parents seldom praised her as they praised her brothers. Nina's father stayed largely silent, except for occasionally erupting at his sons. Her parents generally subscribed to the neglectful parenting notion that children should be seen and not heard.

One day, after being fascinated by a lesson about the solar system, Nina announced to her mother that she wanted to be an astronomer when she grew up. Her mother corrected her by saying that she might one day marry an astronomer. When Nina insisted that she wished to be an astronomer, not marry one, her mother told her, "You're a smart and sweet girl. If you learn to cook, keep a nice house, and always keep yourself looking nice, you'll marry a good man. Girls aren't supposed to be astronomers, Nina. That's a man's job."

Within the strict gender roles of her family, Nina was Othered. She continued to get high grades and secretly persisted with her goal. Eventually, she received a university scholarship to study astrophysics. Nina was able to convince her parents to let her attend, based on the premise that it was a good opportunity to meet a suitable man. She felt ashamed for lying about her intention, and she also felt shame because she didn't measure up to what her mother expected of her as a woman.

Nina's difficulties continued once she started college. As the only woman in an otherwise all-male cohort, taught exclusively by male faculty, Nina worked hard and performed well academically. Nonetheless, she was continually cast as Other because of her gender. She was bypassed for mentorship opportunities and received much less recognition than her male colleagues did. She dodged unwanted sexual advances by both her peers and a professor, but because she questioned herself and feared the fallout of reporting the harassment, *she didn't tell anyone. Nina persisted by pretending that none of the pressure she felt weighed on her and that she didn't notice the disrespectful attention in a sexist environment.*

Like Nina, we find ourselves yearning to be accepted, included, loved, and validated even in the midst of severe forms of exclusion. We willingly work extra hard in response, ignoring the pain in our lives as we continually strive to overcome adversity.

The challenge we can't overcome is that living with "You must work twice as hard" as a rule in our lives sets standards that are impossible to maintain. Always impeccable in our words and actions, always pulled together to represent what someone else needs us to be, never impatient, and beating ourselves up when we fail to be perfect, we work twice as hard to exist.

In a wider scope, this rule is about the fear of being unloved and alone, so it keeps us giving, doing more, and being all things to all people. When it comes to earning someone's love, we are like Jennifer Hudson in *Dream Girls* singing "And I Am Telling You I'm Not Going." In our jobs, we're on time, every day, as scheduled, dutifully taking on more and more and more with a smile and a "Yes!" For the person with constant problems who needs help, we're putting the coffee on, eager to play therapist and social worker and advocate as we offer the voice of outrage—"Oh how dare they!"—no matter what circumstances are going on for us at the time.

We may be good at pretending we're not exhausted for a period of time. We go on shaming ourselves even as our minds and bodies deplete under the weight we're carrying. We can ignore that the high blood pressure, migraines, anxiety, depression, heart problems, backaches, stomach pains, and all sorts of other maladies are signs that we're slowly killing ourselves. We can deny that we're emotion-eating, drinking our way to health problems, shopping our way into a debt hole, or doing all kinds of things instead of dealing with our problems. We lie to ourselves and claim that seeking external sources of validation, whatever they may be, aren't desperate efforts to feel something. We keep doing more until we're completely broken.

Or we can make another choice. We can see that those who've Othered us enforce this rule so we remain in service to them. We can acknowledge that "You must work twice as hard" is a false idea that we need to follow to *be* worthy of love, acceptance, acknowledgment, and more. In reality, we deserve love and worth, and we can have them as we are. We can realize that working twice as hard to obtain someone else's validation is never going to heal or mend us. This is how we begin the work of dismantling such a destructive force.

External Validation Is a False Promise

If you seek external validation for your worth, you've been making the uphill climb for approval for what seems like forever. No matter how far we climb, how hard we persist even as our bodies age and begin to fail us, we continue. But the top of the mountain remains just out of reach, past the clouds that shroud the goal.

Our peace will only come when we recognize that this summit can never be reached. The secure place we long for, where someone else's approval, love, or validation makes us feel whole, is fictional. Test this for yourselves. Search your memory for a relationship or situation in which you finally won approval from a person or group. Did it remain satisfying for more than a short period? External validation is one of the most tenuous things in the universe. We might climb high in pursuit of it, but it's as solid as the clouds we pass through—ephemeral and fleeting. We can't reach it because the moment we give someone else power over our self-worth by asking them to tell us we matter and are beautiful, lovable, worthy, or whatever else we need to feel convinced, we establish a power imbalance. We surrender a power that ultimately belongs to us. So long as that power is ceded, the power imbalance remains.

Anyone who has fought for love knows what this means. Maybe you fought and you got it. Then the minute you did something human—you needed time to yourself, got angry about dishes in the sink, didn't want sex when the other person did—your mate put you in check. They reminded you who had power in the relationship. In a sense, you thought you got somewhere, but were then kicked off the mountainside to start proving your worth again. Up the mountain you went, trying to regain their approval. Or maybe you found another mountain to climb, as we're big on recreating the same story again and again with different people and situations.

This is also true in family dynamics, work environments, social groups, and other ways we engage people. Another person will love, admire, or support us as long as we're doing something for them. A dominant culture does it by keeping us cast as "the Other who exists in service" to them. The minute we have a need of our own, or the minute we say "No," the love, admiration, and support dry up quickly. In some instances, the validation we seek remains hidden because it's dependent on an expectation someone else placed forever out of reach, which we're trying to live up to. Nina's story illustrates how this works.

> *After her college graduation, Nina found meaningful work at a planetarium. She also met the man who became her husband and the couple adopted two foster children. When Nina and her husband divorced eight years later, her mother insisted that Nina's career had interfered with her marriage (when, in fact, she and her husband had worked an equal number of hours). Nina believed her mother, so after the divorce she found herself playing supermom to "make it up to the kids." She meticulously cleaned and cooked to ensure her household was as orderly as her mother's and her meals as perfectly prepared, in spite of the fact that her mother never worked outside the home while Nina had a full-time job. Meanwhile, she continued to pour herself into her work and never let the stress at home show, lest a colleague assume she was too weak to deal with it all.*
>
> *Her mother died two years after Nina's divorce. In the years that followed, Nina carried the belief that she was disappointment to her mother. Even a decade after her mother had passed, Nina continued to wake up each Saturday morning with her mother's voice in her head saying she was lazy for sleeping in and needed to get up to start the family's laundry.*

We spend so much of our lives working twice as hard for the people around us that we take this as a given, a must for our lives. We're powered by an internal engine that chugs along with the rhythms of must, must, must, must and should, should, should, should. For just a moment, consider what you've done for adults who are capable of doing these things for themselves.

Maybe you're like Nina, living up to an expectation that was never truly suited to you. Just pause, take a deep breath, and really feel this. A thought pattern probably takes you quickly into "If I don't do it, someone will suffer," "If I don't do it, they'll be so disappointed," or "If I don't do it, it won't get done." So you double down on your important role as a fixer. As you consider this, see whether you've sought a level of control over situations by assuming responsibilities that can in fact be shared with others. If so, you're actually training them to give their responsibilities over to you.

Yes, that's right. You're *training* them to treat you this way. While some refer to this as "enabling" behavior, it's actually quite a *disabling* behavior. In essence, it says to another adult, "Don't worry about responsible behaviors. You don't need to contribute to this relationship at the same level I do. I'll carry this for both of us." You're clipping their wings to keep them from flying into danger, but at the same time you're disabling their freedom. It teaches the person that they don't need to show up for their adult responsibilities. They don't need to try, reach, or grow when you're willing to take all responsibility.

This is a learned inequity that comes from our experience as Other. The thought patterns that keep us doing the heavy lifting for everyone around us take root in many parts of our lives. The constant climb up the mountain to reach a mythical belief that we'll obtain wholeness through rescuing others becomes a way of being.

The Constant Climb as a Way of Being

Remember the banyan tree analogy in chapter 1? This is the tree with branches that point downward, eventually becoming trunks themselves. This rule of fear spreads similarly. We become so identified with the commitment to work twice as hard, and the struggle of doing so, that this rule leads to a whole network of behaviors. It is our primary method for interacting with the world. In a sense, we are so addicted to seeing our-selves as *the one who must* for everyone else, we're unable to exist otherwise.

If you've followed this rule for a long time, you may often end up thinking, "If I didn't do all these things, who would I be? I'd be irrelevant." The fear of irrelevance is strong. It comes with a whole lot of musts, including these. You must...

- never say "No."

- have few, if any, boundaries for what you will and won't accept.

- be an expert in making other people happy and making them love you.

- always be a good listener, and never express a need of your own.

- give until it hurts, and never admit that it often does.

- be everyone's role model.

- pretend this life you're living, with these circumstances, is exactly what you want.

- hide that being a rescuer is a mostly empty experience.

- make sure everyone thinks you don't mind the constant intrusion of other people's drama and enjoy the work of trying to solve their problems.

- exist by the rules other people laid out for you.

Undoubtedly, there are others specific to your circumstances. Give yourself a few minutes to jot down the "You must" statements you've been living with in your journal. What emotions do these statements evoke for you? There may be sorrow at the time you've spent pleasing others or sacrificing for them, perhaps in vain. Maybe anger? Anger is a totally reasonable response to a situation in which you've put in so much effort for so little reward. We'll explore the role of anger and resentment more in the next chapter. First, let's use our tools to find freedom from this rule of fear.

GAIN THE CLARITY TO GIVE UP
OBLIGATION AND SHAME

Read through these instructions before beginning the exercise or listen to an audio recording of them at http://www.newharbinger.com/46479. Through meditation, you can clarify and slow the racing thoughts that feed the constant action-reaction cycle of trying to rescue the world. By learning to simply be in the moment, you disrupt the tendency to keep shoulding and musting your way through life. This is the first step to getting off the validation-seeking mountain you work twice as hard to climb. The time you spend in mindful awareness of the moment will help you begin to realize that much of the stuff you do isn't actually buying your way toward happiness or freedom. More space opens for you to realize what it is that *You* truly want.

Just as you did in previous chapters, prepare for a meditation exercise by positioning yourself comfortably, dropping your gaze or closing your eyes, inhaling through the nose, and exhaling through the mouth. Do this for a few moments to still whatever thoughts are spinning in your mind and whatever priorities are trying to compete for attention. Or if you prefer, use dance and music to come into a state of clarity. The point is to free your mind from the weight of working twice as hard.

Using mindfulness to bring your attention into this moment, allow yourself to notice the exhaustion in your body, your spirit, and your whole being. You've spent many years being and doing for everyone and everything, so acknowledge this exhaustion. Pay particular attention to the places where it has concentrated in your body and give those parts the attention they've been needing the entire time you've been using them.

Also notice the pull of old thinking patterns that have looped you into working twice as hard. Your attachment to these thoughts is based in old patterns that formed long ago. Notice them and release them, labeling them "thinking" as they attempt to distract you.

Allow yourself to then focus on people who Othered you so you to work twice as hard to prove your worth. Notice the faces of all whose loads you've been carrying. Include everyone no longer in your life, as there may be an oppressive or abusive person from your past whose mess you still carry. Notice this burden.

Recognize that it's time to give back their shame, lack of worth, negativity, decision not to act for themselves, and whatever else you carry. If you attach guilt to this, know it to be simply the product of old patterns that have kept you locked into obligation. You are now seeking to release these agreements.

As you begin to free yourself from the pull of old thinking patterns and behaviors, and the people and systems who've reinforced them, it may feel at once heavy, freeing, sad, joyous. Note whatever feelings show up for you in the moment without judging. Shame's burden has no place here.

Now speak whatever feels right to you. You might say: "I lay down these burdens." "I need to take care of me." "You can have your shame back." "I'm not taking care of everything and everyone anymore." Then spend a few moments experiencing the significance of this statement.

We take back a powerful right by acknowledging that we're choice-makers. We choose to no longer accept someone else's role for our lives—and someone else's judgment of us as Other. As Nina discovered, choosing freedom opens up the possibility of living without shame.

Nina's exercise took her deep into exploring the roots of her shame. Even as she acknowledged her mother's influence, Nina recognized that the most potent shaming voice was her own. She believed that she didn't deserve a career, that her marriage had failed because of it, that she wasn't a good enough parent or homemaker. Essentially, she was telling herself that she wasn't good enough.

She made a decision not to listen to, nor accept, her shame voice. Previously she followed the twisted logic of self-blame, but when the nagging shame beliefs told her "You should," "You must," and "You'll never," she started asking, "Is that so?" As Nina became more skilled in talking back to shame and interrogating it, the shame voice became weaker and was present much less frequently. When it did show up, the experience was like hearing from a stranger. She knew what to do with it as soon as she realized what it was.

The effort to extricate ourselves from the role we were given to be everyone's rescuer, hero, and caretaker takes time. Successfully doing it in some areas of life may be easier than others. The key is persistence. You have carried this burden for years, so it will take time and effort to learn how to let it go. It can scream to be picked up when others try to keep us in the role of needing to prove ourselves. By continuing to practice a loving, intentional effort to lay down the burdens of working twice as hard—which we picked up to meet our human needs to belong and be seen as worthy—we become freer to live with loving kindness, both to ourselves and others. To move further along this path, we can apply the tool of compassion to the parts of ourselves that have suffered from the uphill climb.

Self-Compassion Lifts the Burdens of Regret

So many instances in our histories have us saying: "How could I have been so stupid?" "How could I have been so blind?" "Why didn't I listen to the signs?" "How did I not realize what was going on?" This is shame reasserting itself in a different form. We beat ourselves up about so much: things we did for love and the sacrifices we made for jerks, ways we genuflected before people when we sought their approval, enabling behaviors that have resulted in long-term consequences for us and the people we enabled, commitments we made that we wish we hadn't. We dwell on all the bad advice we gave, bad decisions we made, bad wastes of time or energy or money. Bad, bad, bad. This is more language of shame, often connected with "should."

Shoulds, bads, regrets. This is so often where we go in retrospect. "If only I could do it over again," we say as we remember. In truth, this is a distortion of reality. Each of us made decisions based on the state we were in, and the tools we had available to us, at the time. If we ignored instincts, it's because we didn't yet realize the need to trust them. We didn't know the language of enabling, disabling, caretaking, and rescuing, so we couldn't see the dynamics behind these behaviors.

Forgiving the past is hard to do when shame is involved. Consider this: Suffering for choices made in the past only robs you of finding peace in the present. You must be here now, right in this moment. This moment is what you have. Life is pretty short—too short to spend in regret.

Whatever you're trying to prove or fix or undo, shame is not the answer. You can begin to forgive yourself.

FIND SELF-COMPASSION BY BEGINNING TO FORGIVE YOURSELF

Do the practice of finding your breath and allow your mind to clear the distracting thoughts and beliefs that are driving you at the moment. Then allow yourself to notice a situation from your past that you loop around in shame or the area of your life that's locked into regret. Invite whichever memory needs your immediate attention to come to the forefront.

Allow yourself to witness this particular episode from your life as an observer, as if watching someone you love deeply experience it. You are an outside observer of the scenes, and you can use the movie exercise from chapter 3 to help you watch the younger you in action. Simply watch the story without intervening in it.

Witness all the players involved and the circumstances.

Then focus on precisely what this younger version of you was seeking. Was it companionship, validation, survival, acceptance?

See what the younger you was working twice as hard to get away from, to earn, or to prove. Observe all the things that propelled your younger self into the situation.

As you watch the incident unfold, hold love for younger you and let it feed curiosity. What choices did this character make? Can you see the logic behind the choices? Were they shaped by particular circumstances? Try to summon some empathy for those circumstances, those choices, and the way the character struggled.

Notice how the character used the power of decision-making to move past the event. Observe the resources that were gained, such as knowledge, sharpened instincts, and new discoveries about the world. Consider whether those resources allowed that scrappy character to become wiser or more prepared to trust their instincts. What were the strengths gained from this experience?

Compassion begins with recognizing the choices that you made when times were desperate. You could only draw on the physical and emotional resources available to you at the time. Understanding this leads to self-forgiveness.

We often struggle to forgive ourselves for things we'd easily forgive in loved ones. As we begin learning to experience ourselves as compassionate witnesses to our stories, we recognize the person who was working to survive. *We were working to survive.* There we were, with whatever odds were stacked against us, climbing up, moving forward, keeping life going. We made the choices and sacrifices we believed were needed, and that's what got us to this point.

Regrets don't serve much purpose. As you complete the exercises in this chapter, if you find yourself ruminating on regrets, that means you have work to do. Perhaps there's unfinished grief to tend. Maybe there was a person or opportunity you passed over because you were too busy climbing uphill to really see what was going on around you. If so, this may be the time to creatively address your regrets. When someone you feel regret around is deceased, it's time to consider that they would probably want you to feel compassion for yourself now. After all, your shame serves no purpose for them.

Compassion toward ourselves is especially difficult when we're trying to change patterns of behavior that have kept us locked into hurtful ways of being for a long time. Yet giving ourselves compassion is the method for seeing the "you must work twice as hard" mountain for what it is—an illusory belief borne from our own history and fear. Whatever situations we created as a result of this rule, we now have the choice to climb down the mountain and leave it behind.

Make Music with Your Life

As we begin freeing ourselves from regret, we also free up the space to create new chapters for our story. We can create a fresh journey that's not mired in old patterns of thinking and behaving. As we repair our lives, we find that some of the situations we've placed ourselves in—like relationships that don't give us half of what we put in or dead-end jobs we're dependent on to pay bills—aren't so easy to change. We've climbed so high up the mountain toward an imagined goal that we now wonder how to climb back down.

The creative brain is something to marvel. Just as making art and music expands our conscious awareness of what's possible in these art forms, pulling together the resources we need to extricate ourselves from life situations can expand our awareness of what's possible for our lives. This is the space in which drawing from the places of where we want to be, what we want to do next can help attract us. To do this, here's an exercise to help guide you down the mountain.

UNLEASH CREATIVITY TO TAKE STEPS TO FREEDOM

Begin by centering yourself in meditative breath. Then allow your mind to locate an area of your life where you've worked twice as hard, but feel caught in a struggle that's doesn't offer an easy way out. Pay close attention to that sense of struggle and the hold it has on you.

Notice how this situation holds you in place. Maybe it's a commitment you made to someone, perhaps there are financial obligations. Whatever comes to you, clarify all that seems to keep you climbing this particular mountain.

Imagine what your life will be like once you're free of this obligation—or at least free of its most burdensome parts. Become clear on your yearnings, whether for joy, movement, accomplishment, adventure, or whatever else is there. Allow yourself to feel attracted to the things you yearn for. What's calling to you?

Consider the resources you have now: the faces that light up the moment you say "I need your help" or the physical resources, like money, an empty room in your house, or hours to fill. What resources could you seek out? Let yourself feel drawn to the resources.

Then experience the reality you are moving toward. Write a short story, in the present tense and in the third person, about this new thing you're about to do. Here are some samples to inspire you.

- Virginia is finally back in school! She has overcome her fear of being the oldest person in class and is engaging in vibrant class-room discussions.

- Marco is a free man! He overcame his fear of being alone and broke to create a new life that is uplifting. Instead of constantly feeling guilty and accused by a master manipulator, he is sur-rounded by people who support his dream of starting a business.

- Loysa is once again crafting in her spare room. She overcame her fear of abandonment to make it clear to her twenty-eight-year-old son that she expects him to pay rent or move out. She both accepts his decision to move out and gains an important part of her life back. She is also helping her son experience his power as a choicemaker.

If you have the space and privacy, create a vision board with pictures and encouraging sayings to offer reminders of your goals and to keep them on track. A password-protected file or private Pinterest board and Instagram account can function the same way. Creating a pictorial representation of your plan helps to further shape it. You can draw your vision out, write it as poetry, or choose any medium to represent it. It's your plan and you get to design it.

The good news about this kind of path is that you can modify it along the way. We get to choose, create, respond, adapt. Learning to trust freedom is one of the most empowering gifts we can give ourselves.

So far in this chapter, you've recognized the mountain for what it is. You've seen how your experiences as Other instilled a sense that you needed to keep climbing it. You've examined the experiences you had as you climbed the mountain, recognizing the choices you made—good and bad—based on the information and resources you had at the time. You know that you can draw on resources to choose what you want for your future. You've also opened up to your right to choose, and discovered and mapped a path that can bring you down from the mountain to redirect toward the things you truly care about. Now you get to be sassy and sashay on down that mountain to express *You*, the fabulous person that you are.

Sass Your Way to What You Want

Being sassy is about having the audacity to break cycles. It's about moving boldly into the new—which, while scary, isn't really about a devil you know or don't know, as others might have you believe. It's about owning the right to be a choicemaker and taking the bold steps to do the things you reflected on. Sass will help you achieve your vision.

One of the most significant shifts that occurs at this level of work is beginning to disrupt some significant power structures in your life. This isn't going to be easy to accept for the people who've benefited from you working twice as hard, whether that's your boss, a member of your household or close social network, or anyone around you who shows up at your doorstep with their problems. However, it's time for you take this step on this journey to freedom.

CLAIM SASS AND MAKE YOUR PLAN A REALITY

Begin with a clearing set of meditation breaths to center yourself in a state of stillness without distraction. Reflect on the area of your life you identified in the Exercise to Find Self-Compassion by Beginning to Forgive Yourself—the past choices you regret and where you feel shame about not working hard enough. Then bring to mind the story of what you really want to be doing, which you wrote down in the last exercise.

Hold these two images together, envisioning a split screen that on one side reflects where you need compassion, and on the other reflects your creative vision for your life. One of the most compassionate things you can do for yourself is to follow through on your dreams and take a chance on joy. You owe it to the part of you carrying shame for all these years.

Then determine a first move toward that vision. You are going to act on it immediately after you finish reading this chapter. In your journal, reflect on these questions: What will you do in the next week? Who do you need to reach out to for help? What conversations need to take place? Crystallize these initial steps in your mind so you can back away from the role you've been working twice as hard to fulfill, and move toward freedom.

Of course, dreaming is the easy part. Doing is the real test. Any journey starts with the first steps, just like it did for Dorothy when she followed the yellow brick road out of Munchkinland to find the Wizard. In other words, do your thing Dorothy. You're sassy, remember? As a sassy person, you take audacious action for your life. You know that your survival depends on it—and because you know that, you *can* make the bold decision to take those steps. So finish this chapter, then take your first steps to freedom.

The need for bold, audacious effort isn't just for big dreams in life. Of course, if hiking the Appalachian Trail or attending art school in Paris is what you're thinking, I'm all for it. For many of us, this is about making the simple changes in our life structures that will release us from the constant struggle of working twice as hard. We can break the cycle of proving that we deserve to be here.

It's a journey and daily practice to return to the things that matter most to you. After all, you've spent a lifetime learning to work twice as hard to fulfill someone else's requirements for your life. It's such an easy trap to fall into because there are always people and situations that seem to need rescuing and fixing. Because the shame you've felt for so long can be really sticky, it feels hard to extricate yourself. But you don't need to plaster a smile and take someone else's mess on anymore. You have a life to get creative with and you are a choicemaker. You've got what it takes!

CHAPTER 7

"Oh, You Shouldn't Feel Resentful!"

People who have Othered you probably provide direction on how you should think and feel in response. Our feelings confuse them, because people who've enacted shaming, violence, and extreme oppression on us are surprised that we don't miraculously bounce back. They're surprised that we are scarred by being Othered and still feel the pain. You likely have not "bounced back" from the collective trauma endured by your ancestors' hardships, the effects of which you might still feel down to your bones and may see reenacted over and over again. Yet whatever resentment you've carried has probably been blamed on you. After all, we're supposed to get over this stuff, right? They say: "I meant well." "We didn't know any better." "It was a different time." "Forgive and forget."

Yet we *do* experience resentment. Being Othered is not something we just get past, particularly when the things that harmed us are still happening. To acknowledge this is to become free of the dark places, which continue harm to our psyches, where resentment resides. Whether this rule of fear is especially dominant in your life or it shows up only occasionally, you'll benefit from examining how it came to be in your life and how its presence influences your experience.

This particular rule differs from the previous three because its influence can be more subtle. We easily recognize all the times we worked twice as hard to prove ourselves, have love, or earn a living. Similarly, we hear the voices of our parents, communities, and whomever else instructed us to tone it down, then shamed us for crying out because others are so much worse off than we. We perceive the way we internalized these voices and the experiences that led us to feel Other, and the way our inner critic constantly snipes at us about our desires for something better than the hell that was our status quo.

For most of us, the fourth rule of fear doesn't operate at such an obvious level. Rather, it exists at the very edges of our awareness, containing a story of hidden resentment that we're not always entirely conscious of feeling. This is often accompanied by the sense of helplessness to effect change that accompanies Otherness. Ernest's story helps illustrate this.

Ernest was not formally diagnosed with attention deficit and hyperactivity disorder (ADHD) until his mid-twenties. Instead, he grew up labeled by teachers and fellow students as a "problem" for his classroom behavior. Whether it was wiggling in his seat, shouting out answers, or focusing on anything but the task at hand, he spent much of his school years being disciplined in one form or another. In tenth grade, he dropped out.

The first time he was Othered was in second grade. A teacher, fed up with Ernest's disruptive and distracting behavior, sent him to a school isolation room. It was the first of many school days he'd spend there, separated from his peers. When he complained to his parents, Ernest was told it was important for him to "learn the lesson" and sit still in class. However, the lesson wasn't one he was able to learn. With the exception of band—where he could express a talent for both alto and soprano saxophones—Ernest was not being taught with methods that were useful for him.

Undiagnosed and therefore untreated for ADHD, over the next few years he was placed in the social isolation room over and over again. His teacher's banishment signaled to the other students that Ernest was a nuisance. He began noticing eyerolls, palms being slapped against foreheads, and other small but dramatic actions that the children used to publicly register annoyance with him in class. During recess, they banished him from games altogether or ganged up to heap their collective shaming on him. As the years went on, Ernest grew more and more humiliated, confused, and angry. When the school began restricting him from band activities, Ernest fell into depression. Home was no better. Ernest's parents seemed to collude with the school, treating him like a problem and enforcing similar forms of punishment aimed to improve his academic performance.

It wasn't until Ernest was in his mid-twenties that he was diagnosed with ADHD. He was playing in the local jazz scene and a fellow musician suggested he reach out to a community mental health clinic to address his symptoms of depression. Upon receiving treatment and information that normalized his diagnoses, his symptoms improved. Although at times he continued struggling to focus on tasks and conversations, and could get distracted by racing thoughts, Ernest was better able to manage his life.

Even as he learned to live with ADHD and thrive through managing his symptoms, Ernest was haunted by memories of being cast out and isolated by teachers, his classmates, and his parents. Everyone had punished him for things he could not change on his own. He resented their cruelty and the fact that they never tried to understand him nor recognized his musical giftedness. He continually found himself asking "Why?"

Like Ernest, have you found yourself asking *why* oppression, bullying, and other social hardships existed in your life? You might still carry resentment toward those who inflicted these obstacles. You recognize how their actions helped usher you toward struggles with your worth as a person and deep despair may have become a shadow presence in your life. You may also resent the things you were denied in the process, including recognition of your gifts.

This *why?* you're asking, or even demanding in outrage over the ludicrous mistreatment you experienced through Othering, is what we're here to address. True, no answer can provide logical justification for mistreating a child nor for being treated as "less than" today. But addressing *why?* can help you take action for your mental health.

This work continues the journey to freedom from someone else imposing terms for our self-worth and well-being. As choicemakers, we can unpack our reactions to the people whose privilege keeps them from seeing us as equal. We can encounter our normal reactions and own our resentment *so that it does not own us.* By becoming clear about all the anger and resentment we hold—even if we've attempted to disown it or perhaps channeled it into distractions that ultimately depleted our bodies and spirits—we can reshape resentment into a source for change. To begin doing this, we need to understand the role resentment has played in our lives.

Looking at Old Resentments

Resentment is our natural human response to cumulative injustice. We're as wired to resent injustice as a beagle is wired to follow a scent. It's there to tell us, "Hey there. Time to change these circumstances before you're consumed by them." It exists to keep us moving through actions that range from taking part in activism that addresses inequity to walking out the door on a bad relationship. Resentment is best understood as a *healthy and normal response* to unjust circumstances.

The key to using resentment as positive fuel is to be willing to recognize the layers of our resentments and name them. When Ernest reflected on his school and family life, he saw that he resents the mistreatment he experienced for circumstances that were entirely outside his control. The more we can clearly specify the parts of ourselves that still rage against our persecutors of the past, the better prepared we are to finally heal these old wounds.

To heal, we cannot erase the past, pretend it didn't happen, or go on as if it doesn't still affect us. Working to restore ourselves after years spent hurting from, and resenting, the past is an experience I liken to the Japanese art form *kintsugi*. When broken pieces of pottery are repaired with gold or silver lacquer, the effect is a fully repaired bowl or carafe. While a fine piece of pottery on its own, a kintsugi piece is made beautiful and extraordinary by the golden or silver seams along the fractures. In much the same way, we bring together the parts of our life that are chipped, broken, and fragmented. As we do, our whole person emerges threaded with gold along points that were previously broken, reflecting the beauty and strength we've poured into our own repair work.

We've been broken, and have felt the pain of brokenness. As we do deep healing work, we are stronger, more beautiful, and possess true refinement. For we too become woven with gold in the very places we once thought ourselves broken. To prepare for this level of repair and strengthening work, we'll explore how resentments show up in present-day circumstances.

Clarify Your Understanding of Current Resentments

Look at your present life and notice resentment you've felt in recent times or may be experiencing today. Some of these are probably easy to understand: you had a terrible relationship with a boss, person you dated, or spouse. Perhaps a friend or family member betrayed you. Microaggression may have trivialized your contributions, intellect, or status—and accumulated over time. Or a singular injustice continues to cause a lot of hurt. You also rightfully resent the shootings, erasure of human rights, and health and social disparities experienced by your community and those you love.

Those are the resentments you can see. But do you ever find yourself resenting people for reasons that are hard to pinpoint? Perhaps they did nothing wrong to you themselves or they might be a celebrity who's not in your personal life. But because of some aspect of their character, you find yourself resenting them.

To help you see this hidden aspect of resentment, think of the word "privileged" and let a picture of someone's face come to mind. Really bring that image into focus, concentrating it on an individual, whether someone you know, a stranger, a celebrity, a leader of some sort. As you notice the image, pay attention to things this individual seems to have that you've been denied: freedom, benefits, opportunities, social advances, healthcare, whatever comes to mind. Maybe they have moved through life oblivious to struggles you, or people you care about, have known.

With this image still in mind, notice associations you make about the person's character: clueless, destructive, greedy, gluttonous, whatever arises. Notice if part of your resentment has to do with the power this individual holds, relative to your own. Their power, whether vested by social status, race, gender, or another factor of inequality, has been disturbing enough for your life to feel unsettled. This sense of disturbance is likely kicked up when you encounter people who seem to possess these traits you resent. Here's how this occurred for Ernest.

Even as he forged a meaningful adult life and became involved in a long-term relationship, Ernest reacted strongly to bullying behavior. When encountering aggressive drivers on the road, he would sometimes fly into a rage. He had a tendency to personalize issues at his work. When Ernest didn't believe that musicians were being treated fairly, he fumed during interactions with club owners and music promoters because he believed he was hearing disrespect. He also registered instant dislike for anyone who said they don't read the news or pay attention to political issues, because Ernest felt they were "choosing not to give a damn about the rest of the world." He frequently got into arguments on social media.

By registering instant dislike, perceiving bullying in aggression, and feeling disrespected, Ernest navigated a large portion of his life in a state of conflict. But by engaging in arguments and raging against bad drivers, Ernest ultimately gave the choice of his wellness to other people. He had old wounds and scars of Otherness that he carried from childhood experiences of helpless humiliation from being cast out and bullied by people in an uncaring education system. These reactivated in the present day whenever he encountered anything he perceived as bullying and ignorance. To explore how resentment may show up for you, perhaps in ways you don't actually see as resentment, we'll engage the clarity tool.

GAIN CLARITY ON WHAT RESENTMENT IS TRYING TO TELL YOU

Because you'll do this activity while engaged in a deep-breathing mindfulness practice, before you begin read through the instructions and grab whatever you're using to journal. You can also listen to an audio recording that will guide your process at http://www.newharbinger.com/46479.

Once you're ready, bring your mind to a space of stillness, using the deep-breathing or dance method you prefer. By this point, you've learned what works to clear your mind of life distractions: the to-do lists, the shoulds, the judgements about whether you're doing exercises right or not. Clarity is a personal experience, and within mental silence whatever comes to you is what you need in the moment. By first clearing the mind, you can encounter what really needs attention.

Scan your awareness and notice what part of your particular Otherness story gets your attention each time you've encountered the word "resentment" in this chapter.

As you bring the matter into focus, rather than just feeling how it impacts you, call to mind all the people involved in this situation, with all its dimensions. Who or what has contributed to Othering you? What resentment are you experiencing right now as you picture them? If this brings you into contact with deep resentments for ancestral suffering that still shows up for you in the treatment of people in your race or culture today, go there. You honor them with this reflection.

As you scan this story, notice what resentment costs you. Think and journal about this in two ways: 1) Identify what these people and this situation have taken from you that you resent and 2) Consider what feeling this way is costing you, physically, emotionally, psychologically. What is being lost to resentment?

The resentment you're experiencing is here to tell you what you want or need that you're not getting right now, and that you haven't been getting since you first began to experience Othering. What does resentment reveal about what's missing? Be specific as you write down the details in your journal.

When we do resentment work, we begin to get in touch with all the deep rage from being Othered. Importantly, it provides an opportunity to articulate how it has felt from the perspective that this rage is ordered and natural. In other words, we were supposed to pretend that the problem was ours to fix, or something we had no choice but to accept. We were not supposed to see that Otherness was something done to us or forced on us in a broken society, a broken family, a broken school system, and all the other places injustices show up. Then we awaken and realize all the lies about ourselves that we've believed, all the shame we've carried as a result, all the plates of "less than" that we were served up while someone else feasted, and all the fear that kept us flagellating and shaming ourselves. As we awaken to these realities, our righteous anger emerges.

This is a stage of griefwork. It's healthy to be angry over injustice inflicted on you, particularly when it has you believe that you deserve, and should accept, less. Welcome anger, as it takes the place of self-blame within the process of grieving your story of Otherness. Anger arises when body and soul are awakening from the crippling hell of shame and defeat.

Ways to Keep the Anger Healthy

Anger is very tricky. It's easy to halt inner work at the anger stage because it can feel powerful and seductive. People fear anger, and what they fear, they avoid. When that happens—when people see your anger and back down or when they begin to defer to you instead of expecting you to defer to them—the roles seem to reverse so *you're* the one who's in control. Or at least, it feels that way. But what the dominant culture fears, it will also oppress by any means necessary.

While strategic displays of anger can help us teach bullies, oppressive people, and institutions that they'd best not cross us, anger doesn't always stop there. We can end up carrying the fire of our anger into everyday interactions, as Ernest did, where it's provoked but perhaps also misplaced. For example, aggressive drivers are sometimes just late for work, rushing to the hospital, or personally stressed, and probably not trying to bully us specifically. Personalizing other people's stress and making it about us creates unintended consequences. You may be the one who pays the price of those consequences.

We can carry anger into relationships that could otherwise be healthy and growth-promoting. Anger at a lifetime of Othering can leave us feeling very guarded around people who trigger us to encounter old scars. We see the parts of them we associate with our historical oppressors. A loud male boss, for example, could have a voice and demeanor that reminds us of a loud male figure who degraded us in our past. We attribute all sorts of negative qualities to this person in our present circumstances, walling ourselves off from them and their influence. As a result, we can miss ideas, support, or whatever else they have to offer.

We do this because we have so much resentment built up around what this person represents to us that we cannot see the individual through their race, gender, sexual identity, economics, or other features that remind us of those who Othered us. As a result, they also miss out on contributions we could have made to their lives.

Sometimes we go into situations anticipating another person's rejection of us, and therefore reject them first. Or we test them to see at what point they'll reject us, making coexistence impossible. We can carry so much resentment that we even block out the people who love and care most about us. That firewall of anger, which we use so we never feel vulnerable, can burn out of control and hurt people we love.

It's important to understand resentment so we can begin to heal from the pain it inflicts. If you live with so much fire that you're burning down your own house, you need a new way to channel it. You have identified what resentment says you truly need, whether that's basic safety, recognition, respect, dignity, love, empathy, or anything under the sun. This need reveals how you can channel resentment: If you resent isolation and need connection, you can seek the love of your people in a very clear and intentional way. If you resent irrelevance and oppression, you may need solidarity with friends and allies who are committed to helping you carry the struggle. If you feel held back by your resentment, you may need to simply *let go*—to take the energy you've devoted to resentment and use it for something different, something new.

In other words, resentment points you to something missing from your life right now that stands in opposition to the mistreatment you've endured. We'll use our remaining tools to channel your anger and resentment so you don't get stuck in it, burning yourself and those you love.

Compassionately Hone Your Natural Instincts

Self-compassion isn't a simple mind game to convince yourself that you're okay. Rather, it's about honoring the path you've been traveling all this time. It's a way to recognize your struggle, in terms of both what you couldn't do *and* what you could and did do. Compassion is what we experience in the precise moment when we open up to saying, "Oh yeah, I have walked this path. I have been fierce, wise, and resourceful when I needed to be. And I forgive myself for the times I did things that were very human of me." We can grow even more when we stop acting without thinking, and instead explore what resentment is trying to tell us in the moment.

Fear resides in places of deep yearning, and this is where your resentment is guiding you. Having used resentment to recognize what you need, now you'll use self-compassion to honor the strength you have and the people who show up in your life because you make them want to be there. Resentment has allowed you to locate the wounds, and intentionally experiencing self-compassion will provide the salve. To start, let's explore the parts of resentment that are causing you the most shame.

In our personal lives, we experience a lot of resentment that we wish we didn't have. We resent people and circumstances, then feel ashamed for our feelings. This is especially true when resentment is focused on people we love or wish we could love more fully. Sometimes we resent a person who is sick or dying because our fear of abandonment is kicked to the surface. If a parent or other family member who Othered you throughout your life is passing, we can experience a complex mixture of pity, resentment, satisfaction, and guilt.

It's important to examine the presence of resentment, even when it's subtle. For example, you may feel resentment toward someone who's sick and requires more attention than you wish to give, or than you believe they deserve. Maybe you resent a spouse or partner who loves you, but who seems much happier and more fulfilled in life areas outside your relationship. If you feel guilty and ashamed for what you resent, know that people have resentments of all sorts.

This exercise focuses on the way resentment causes you to experience shame. Remember that resentment, like any emotion, is there to bring an issue into our awareness. Our task now is to address any lingering messages that suggest "I shouldn't resent."

FORGIVE YOURSELF FOR RESENTMENT
WITH SELF-COMPASSION

Begin by taking a few breaths, or doing whatever mental clearing activity works well for you, to clear your mind and deepen your focus. Then concentrate on an area of resentment that is troubling you most. Who do you resent and feel ashamed about resenting? While it may feel hard to name someone, try to stay present while exploring this distressing experience. Remember this exercise is only for you, so there's no need to feel shame in this private moment.

As you bring the person to mind, allow the relationship to come into view. Perhaps it is a typical incident that exemplifies the relationship and the aspect of it that you've felt ashamed for resenting.

What did you give this relationship to feed and nurture it? Think about all you've brought to the relationship, all that you invested, all the emotional energy you poured in.

What have you been needing from this relationship that it's not giving you now, or perhaps has never given you? Drill down to the basic human need you have that this relationship is not supplying in its current form. Is it security, companionship, validation?

- Get very clear on what you need, but aren't getting, and make it a statement. Here are some examples.

- "I need love and companionship, and you can't give that to me anymore because you passed away and left me here."

- "I need security, and you've taken that away from me by losing your job."

- "I need you to acknowledge that you really wronged me when I was growing up. I needed you to be a loving parent, yet you Othered me."

- "I need to feel fulfilled as a parent too. I carried your children and am raising them, but you get to be the fun parent and don't show up for the rest."

- "I need to feel I'm actually getting somewhere in my career. You take advantage of my willingness to work twice as hard as I try to prove that I'm worth a promotion."

Whatever your statement is, this is what you really need but aren't getting, or perhaps it's something historical that you did not get when you needed it. Once the statement is clear in your mind, close your eyes and breathe. Repeat this "I need" statement, noticing how important it is in your life and why it's there. Most importantly, notice the humanness behind it.

As we start to strip away the layers of *should-shame,* which is the tendency to tell ourselves what we should and should not be feeling, we can understand the essence of our needs. You feel resentment in a situation because you need something for survival and well-being. It takes a powerful person to look at their life without flinching and to specify what they need right now. Here's how Ernest did this.

Ernest realized he had unmet needs for justice, ownership, accountability, and recognition. He needed the teachers, his parents, and whoever punished him as a child to acknowledge that the symptoms he'd displayed were outside of his control. Specifically, he resented that his parents didn't advocate for him with the school and instead blamed everything on him.

To address the situation and name what powered his resentment, Ernest developed two needs statements. The first of these was historical, addressed to his parents: "I need you to take ownership of the fact that you blamed me for shit that was out of my control. I have ADHD and it sucked to be in school, treated like an imbecile by so-called teachers. You did nothing. I need you to take ownership for royally screwing up my life." Even as Ernest struggled through the shame of not "getting past" the trauma, which was still with him, clarifying and articulating his needs was a significant healing step toward being able to do repair work with his parents.

Ernest's second needs statement had to do with his present circumstances: "I need to feel respected. I am an artist who brings

*music into the world that makes people happy and free. I need to feel
like I'm heard, like we're heard as jazz artists."*

As Ernest experienced, you may feel selfish or petty for acknowledging historical circumstances. We blame ourselves for not being able to just "get past" old resentments for things that happened long ago. We tell ourselves we should forget about it (even though we haven't) and that the past is the past (except it's still lingering). It's not silly to have resentment. It's perhaps sillier, yet common, to pretend that we have no resentments and then try to manipulate guilt from people who may, or may not, have played a direct role in our mistreatment.

Denying a need doesn't keep it from existing. The need will continue to assert itself. Being honest with ourselves about the need, and resentment's role in it, allows us to make conscious choices so the need gets met. It also prevents cycling through destructive tendencies with people, such as the need to manipulate guilt through sarcasm, passive-aggressiveness, or other behavior tendencies that signal resentment—but not directly. Staying with your truth and being honest in the process keeps us moving into progressively healthier states of being. Creativity provides an opportunity to take this to the next level.

Notably, your resentment work may be taking you back to ancestral trauma—ways those like you were persecuted in situations and dynamics similar to the ones you've experienced. It is normal and natural to resent the brutal subjugation of your ancestors. If this presents itself as part of a prominent need statement, using the tools of creativity and sass will give you a method for responding to this need.

USE CREATIVITY AND SASS TO MAKE WHAT'S BEEN HIDDEN SEEN

For this section, you can journal or use a medium to draw or paint. Read through the instructions before beginning, and then determine how you wish to approach the exercise. Begin by using your preferred mindfulness practice. This process will guide you through seeing how resentment and anger impact your life.

Notice the time you have spent on resentment, the mental energy you gave to people and situations. It may be helpful to envision this as something you've physically expended, like we expend sweat or tears. Pay attention to the physical and emotional toll from all that resentment and see its purpose for your life now.

With resentment as an emotion that exists to get your attention about needs that aren't met, you've become aware of some of these needs. Now consider your history resenting people and circumstances, and the exhaustion from having carried it for a long time. What role do you want resentment to play in your life as you move forward?

Imagine yourself moving through life, no longer needing to give your energy to old resentments. You better understand your relationships with people who once activated your resentment, and the circumstances they represent. With this in mind, choose from the following activity options.

Write a short story or poem about the changes in your present life that will allow you to no longer carry resentment for the past. You can use first or third person. Wherever your resentment work needs to take place, you can use this as story's location.

Write a goodbye letter to people or circumstances you once resented, if you're ready to let them go. When the relationship marked by resentment still exists, specify the terms you now require in order to no longer resent. What changes does the other person need to make to their behavior? What changes do you need made to the situation you're both in? You can decide whether or not you wish to share the letter with the other person—the most important thing is to write it.

Sketch, paint, or use mixed media to make an artistic representation of your changing relationship with old resentments from the past. This could be a representation of you getting stronger from your choice to no longer be silent. Or an image of you containing resentment, as one contains a fire, for use when needed—perhaps if you're ever being actively, deliberately Othered in the present as you were in the past.

WORK WITH RESENTMENT FROM
ANCESTRAL TREATMENT

If you wish to do ancestral work for this activity, give yourself space to notice how resentment of their story is showing up for you now. Begin by sketching the family tree that reflects a legacy of Otherness that you resent. Having their faces in mind can help, but if you don't know what ancestors looked like, it may be helpful to imagine that their faces look like you and people in your immediate family. The mental picture is important, so spend some time envisioning. Then answer these questions.

- When you consider your resentment of ancestral trauma, what message calls out through time to enter your experience today?

- Are you expressing resentment for their suffering in any way that's harming you or those around you—mentally, emotionally, or physically?

- What might your ancestors need you to do differently in honor of their struggle? You have mental images of their faces, so it may be helpful to close your eyes, picture them, and ask.

- In what new ways can you honor your ancestors as you move forward? Describe these in ways that feel real and necessary. Perhaps you envision yourself standing among them in their most oppressed state, looking forward into your future. Or leap a year down the road from your present life, when you have honored their memory and healed the lingering resentment, and ask what was needed. Do whatever works for you.

As we begin to understand the role resentment has played in our lives, we perceive the choices we need to make. Whereas there are innumerable situations, past and present, that we cannot change directly—that certainly include other people's behaviors—we get to choose how much power we still give those situations. Although you may resent someone who has power over you, which you may not have the ability to change, you do get to set the terms. Their power does not have to include your every waking thought, your health, and other things you may be handing over to them right now. Here's how Ernest worked through this.

Ernest determined that he no longer wished to stew in old resentments that caused misunderstandings and present-day hurt with his parents. Ernest admitted that he wanted them to hear his truth about how their negligence had allowed him to be harmed. He recognized that such a conversation could have a number of outcomes: they could accept his truth and express regret, declare they lacked information on ADHD or deny its existence, or perceive his words as blame and become angry with him. He had to contemplate whether his need to feel heard was worth the consequences.

As he contemplated, Ernest admitted to himself that old habits of holding resentment, not expressing it, and then using sarcasm or explosiveness in his adult relationship with his parents did not serve him. By admitting this, he took responsibility for his resentment instead of allowing it to continue controlling him. He decided to ask his parents about their experience raising him so he could gain a better understanding of what they had dealt with. This would allow him to determine what he could bring up, and how.

As Ernest learned to operate with a theme of respect, expecting it in all his interactions, he was able to meet his need specifically. Rather than raging when he saw Othering behavior occur around him, he could draw on his own experience. When his nephew Kaito was diagnosed with dyslexia and ADHD, Ernest was able to coach his sister and her husband to advocate for their child's educational needs. At the forefront of Ernest's message to them was, "Kaito needs to feel respected and know that he's just as capable and deserving as every other kid at that school."

Most importantly, Ernest came to recognize that people like his parents, professionals in the music industry, and his sister and brother-in-law have their own lives and choices. Some had wronged him in the past—but he, as a choicemaker, made the decision to no longer act from old resentments, nor put himself into situations that he'd eventually resent. Ernest adopted a mantra: "What do I need to do in this situation now so that I'm not resentful later?"

We need to give our instincts their rightful place as sources of information for our lives. We can recognize our capacity to consider this information in ways that support what is healthiest and best for us, and the people around us, then *decide* how we'll act on it. When you learn to clarify the places within you that feel lacking and neglected, the parts of yourself that have chafed for too long in a life spent feeling Othered, you can get in touch with your instincts again, owning your capacity to act as you choose. In doing so, you create the potential for a life that is authentic, fulfilling, and a reflection of you being your best.

Resentment is a deep emotion that exists within our natural reaction to being cast out as Other. So much of the time, we disown resentment or fail to name it. Yet we act from it, we feel it, but we don't comprehend what it means for our lives. As we wake up to resentment's message, it helps us see what we're missing and shows us the way to fulfill a basic need we have.

Through becoming clearer on our needs, we start to remove obstacles. Or we choose a different path that allows us to restore dignity. By taking steps toward these important choices in our lives, we begin to rely less on resentment. After all, resentment's role is minimized when the things we long for and the basic rights we have are acknowledged. And we, as choicemakers, have the right to fulfilling lives.

CHAPTER 8

"You Cannot Change the World"

This is the rule of despair. It arises from a dark pit of beliefs telling us that in spite of all the work we do, things will stay the same. We can speak truth, advance our lives, and leave behind people and circumstances that no longer fit—changing some things in our lives, in small ways. But the significant choices—the choices that really matter—have already been made for us by a world that is how it is and cannot be changed. This rule tells us that we began as Othered people and, ultimately, that's what we'll remain.

The belief that the world is a hard and unchanging place where the path for our lives has been set, so it's impossible to change course, is hard to escape. Social inequity is a constant struggle that we see all around us and experience directly. From proud displays of hate symbols intended to intimidate, to any person or government entity or institution choosing who gets served and who gets condemned, to shootings, hate crimes, and human-made disasters—all leave us feeling hopeless. Even the most optimistic among us are challenged.

A few summers ago, I was enjoying fireworks at a friend's house. He pointed at a nearby home that displayed its owner's prosperity. "The guy's a plumber," he said. Instinctively, one of the women told her ten-year-old daughter, "Marry a plumber when you grow up." I smiled in the girl's direction and suggested, "Or maybe she'll want to be a plumber when she grows up." The woman's response? "No one would ever hire a female plumber."

After all, you cannot change the world. To this woman, men are plumbers, not women, and that is that. What's more, it is inconceivable that anyone could think differently. I disagree with her assertion, not only because I did an online search and found evidence to the contrary, but also because it's based in an untruth that sexism taught us all to believe.

Plenty of people still accept this particular untruth about women's abilities, particularly women of color and transwomen, to insist they cannot be electricians, surgeons, astronauts, sportscasters, or government leaders in spite of very clear evidence and examples that show otherwise. Sexism, along with racism, ableism, heterosexism, classism, fatphobia, and transphobia have attempted to instill beliefs that we all have the ability to decontaminate.

As ingrained as these patterns may be and as deeply as we experience hopelessness, something living deeper within us serves as a counterargument. We see persistence in the stories that inspire us and we are inspired to persist as well. We create change each day by asserting our aspirations and exercising our right to occupy professions, neighborhoods, academic institutions, and public spaces that were off limits to people like us not too long ago. Some of these spaces may still be largely off limits today. Against the odds, we still show up.

That doesn't mean we're not riddled with self-doubt as we come face-to-face with people and systems that don't seem to agree with our right to realize our life visions. This feels particularly immediate when we look around and see so few like us. In such moments, we might ask, "Why am I here doing this thing?" and start to question ourselves. We feel like imposters, to the extent that we sabotage our own success because we don't quite believe we're supposed to have it. As this pattern of ours starts to have impact, back we go—down into despair. We start to believe we can't change the world we live in nor our ultimate fate within that world.

Change is possible. It's not easy—but it's possible. Our task is to do all we can to work toward, and win, the lives we all deserve, by virtue of our humanity. To do this, we need to recognize the fear and self-doubt that occur in response to witnessing how intractible the world's systems of oppression seem to be. This way, we don't become trapped and cycle back into defeat each time we rise. To help you see these tendencies, we'll dive into each part of our defeat experience, beginning with feeling like an imposter.

Why We Feel Like Imposters

One of the mind-tricks the world plays on us has us think that no matter what we do to advance our lives, we will always be Other. Even with all the work we've done to improve our self-worth and accept the fabulous beings that we are, when it comes time to translate that internal change into external action, we still enter spaces where our differences once again confront us. In these moments, old Otherness tapes start playing in our heads. We find ourselves in a world apart, feeling separate and isolated. The culture and ways of being we are trying to function within are foreign to us.

What you encounter in these moments is called *imposter phenomenon* (Clance and Imes 1978). If you ever feel like a phony or fear being called out as a fraud despite any accomplishment, and experience isolation and a sense of nonbelonging, this is likely what's happening. It can lead us to question ourselves to the point that we revert to old rules of fear, like toning down our individuality and working twice as hard to prove our right to be there. Chinh's story helps illustrate this.

> *As the son of a Vietnamese sex worker and an American serviceman, Chinh was eligible for immigration to the US after the Vietnam war. A well-off Vietnamese couple purchased Chinh's immigrant rights from his birth mother in order to come to America with Chinh, when he was two. Chinh's memories of his early years were saturated with feeling empty and confused in his adoptive parents' home as they established their new life.*
>
> *The neighborhood school he attended was ethnically diverse. Chinh's physical features from his multiracial background still made him stand apart, and social outings with his family reinforced his sense of being an outsider. Within the Vietnamese community that formed their social circle, Chinh stood out from the monoracial kids his age. Meanwhile, outside of Asian communities, he was only seen as Asian—and thus, Other—subject to epithets and pejorative references to his native language.*

With this sense that he didn't belong, and that he was different from everyone around him, Chinh grew into adolescence with a question: "Who am I?" His only knowledge of his birth mother came with the epithets that his adopted parents used to describe her. He deduced that his biological father was a White serviceman, but even his adopted parents could supply no further details. Chinh developed a yearning for acceptance that other kids took advantage of, seizing upon his strong desire for approval.

Dating proved equally challenging. Asian parents, suspecting the origins of Chinh's birth and immigration, did not allow their daughters to date him. Non-Asian girls laughed whenever he mustered the courage to ask one out. They called him Long Duk Dong, in reference to the character in the film Sixteen Candles.

Chinh fell into a depression that made it a struggle to get out of bed and continue with daily activities. Chinh's parents blamed him for this, while pressuring him to perform academically. He wanted to please his parents, so he also pressured himself to succeed. He never felt like their child, and in private they made it clear he wasn't. He often felt like a fraud, as if playing a role for his parents' friends and everyone at school. He also saw successes in school as the result of continued pressure to maintain the role his parents laid out for him.

This continued in college. His scholarship added pressure to play what he saw as "the smart Asian kid who doesn't get into trouble." Chinh felt confined to a stereotype of Asian college kids, his individuality unrecognized and his need to feel seen unacknowledged. In spite of achievement that was earned—he was scholarly and did perform well in school—he struggled to feel a sense of belonging or purpose, and experienced deepening depression.

Like Chinh, we can have a sense of being imposters. When we exist in spaces that aren't welcoming, or that make the welcoming contingent on whether we live within a narrow set of expectations, playing roles can take over. So long as we're assuming our role—whether that's "the smart Asian kid," "the listener," "the troubleshooter with no needs of her own," "the rescuer of others' feelings," "the guy who laughs at jokes made at his expense," "the forgiver of oppression"—we get the stamp of approval. For the privileged attempt to define the terms for our existence and the role we play.

In some instances, our feelings of rejection have been accurate. We question why we're there because people create a climate that causes us to wonder. Somehow, our questioning is treated with hostility, and we're gaslit into believing that a hostile environment isn't really hostile, and that this is all in our heads. No wonder we feel like imposters!

All this time that we spend feeling like imposters and trying to live up to the unrealistic expectations that result from having to play a complicated role, we're not seeing our talents, our gifts, our contribution. We then fall into becoming dependent on praise and requiring assurance that we're okay, that we belong and are acceptable. Sometimes we swing to the other extreme, assuming that praise means someone is patronizing us, brownnosing, or trying to make us feel better out of pity.

The more centered in our own truth we can be, recognizing the value we bring just as we are, we become more able to accept praise at face value. This allows us to be more open and receptive to constructive feedback, able to draw the line and say "No" to feedback intended to demoralize us, and accurately tell the difference between what our histories of Otherness might tell us is happening and what is actually happening.

We're all equal. We have to choose to live as equals and stop waiting for permission to show up. Folks may not have a lot of experience interacting with people from your background, your culture, your identity, your ways of being. Well, now is the time for them to gain this experience.

Still, just at the point when a dream is about to be realized, a goal reached, hard work and travail about to pay off, we can self-sabotage. When we've been Othered long enough, success seems perilous and we come to feel we are somehow destined to fail.

The Human Tendency to Sabotage Our Lives

The tendency to self-sabotage is such a common method of defeating ourselves that Virgil and Ovid were writing about it more than two thousand years ago. It's powerfully captured in the Greek myth about Orpheus and Eurydice, which I'll retell briefly. Orpheus and Eurydice are in love. She dies and goes to the underworld for dead souls. Orpheus is heartbroken and embarks on a major journey to the underworld, where his story of love and the enchanting music he plays on his lyre convinces Queens Persephone and King Hades of the underworld to release Eurydice. Hades gives one condition: She can follow Orpheus to the mortal world, but he must proceed forward and not look back. If he looks back even once to be sure that Eurydice is following, she'll remain in the underworld forever. So, of course, he looks back at just the moment when they finally arrive at the gate leading out of the underworld. Poof! There she goes, back to the land of death, where she must remain forever.

We get it. Orpheus did that oh-so-human thing. He could not proceed with faith that his beautiful love song had truly convinced Hades to release Eurydice. He had to test it. And so, after all that work to get to the underworld to retrieve her, he sabotaged his happiness and the opportunity to have what he wanted most.

The human tendency is to let doubt overrule faith, thereby sabotaging our own success. We doubt our ability to have an impact, create change for ourselves, be truly happy, and more. In essence, we doubt the power of our own choicemaking. Often, our doubt reaches full strength at the moment just before the goal is reached.

At this point, we get anxious, suspicious that it's not really happening, and we wait for the other shoe to drop. Rather than face the possibility of disappointment and failure, or having a terrifyingly unfamiliar experience of good fortune and success, we decide it's better to take ourselves out of the game. So we do. We call it quits on the hard work we've been devoting to our education, our health goal, our career aspiration. If we don't stop the work entirely, we begin devoting less attention to it until someone else notices that it's sloppy. The result is a poor grade, demotion, termination, or "thanks, but no thanks" message.

Self-sabotage shows up in our relationships too. People bring us joy, and we bask it in for a time. Then we question it. We expect it will come to end so we test it. Perhaps we think we don't deserve this person, so we test them to make sure we're right. We start retreating into some of our most destructive behaviors to see if the other person will still love us. Then they set boundaries, say no, react with their own destructive behaviors, or leave altogether. In this way, we've sabotaged something healthy and whole because we didn't know what to do with the good stuff.

Most of these activities are unconscious. You probably never said to yourself, "Wow, the due date is six months away, but they'll never let me reach it anyway. Time to check out to avoid being rejected when I get there." You definitely weren't consciously saying, "Our lives are going so well. Look at her sleeping there like an angel. She really trusts me. Time to test that trust because someone like me doesn't deserve love."

Yet this is precisely what happens when the underlying belief is based in the rule of fear that you cannot change the world. We have so much doubt in our ability to create the changes we want for our lives and to improve our circumstances. We doubt our rights and ability to be happy, reach goals, and experience success, so we create "evidence" to back up our assertions. We self-sabotage, activating this rule of fear so it fulfills our doubts. As a result, the failure happens. The relationship ends. The goal is not reached. Sometimes we manage to weave such predicaments that things can no longer be reached or repaired. After all, what's the use of self-sabotage if we don't burn the bridge afterward?

After we've self-sabotaged, we experience hindsight. In Greek mythology, this was the domain of the Titan Epimetheus. If we're able to be honest with ourselves, as we look back we can see how we sabotaged our lives through choices, made at each juncture, that resulted in the collapse of our dream. This leads us into despair—a common landing point after we become mired in the belief that we cannot change the world. Let's explore despair a bit more so that when you apply your tools, the path out of it will be clearer.

Understanding the Texture of Despair

Despair has deep roots in our worldview. It's the feeling we get from being in a state of self-defeat: believing that, try as we might, we have no real ability to create change. There are many parts to our despair that feed off each other, taking us into its depths.

We live with a great challenge. There are human atrocities occurring all around us, and some of them impact us directly. As we live with these things, then combine them with the struggle to get up and face each day, it's easy to see how despair can weigh on even the most optimistic among us. This is what happened to Chinh.

> After struggles with college that included heavy drinking—which caused long-term health concerns—Chinh graduated, began his career, and developed a social network of people who shared his interest in gaming. He fostered a distant but cordial relationship with his adopted parents, maintaining a commitment to look after them as they aged. Direct assaults grew less frequent, limited to brief encounters in which Asian pejoratives were used to Other him.
>
> Then the COVID-19 pandemic broke out. Seemingly overnight, Chinh noticed shifts in people's behaviors in grocery stores and on the streets. He caught stares that suggested a mixture of suspicion and loathing. One day, while walking home from the bus stop, a man spat in his face and screamed accusations at Chinh about bringing "the Chinese virus." For the first time since childhood, Chinh became fearful for his safety. Continuing news feeds reported other Asians in America being attacked on the streets, which fed his despair. His old cycle of depression started once again.

Chinh's story illustrates the burden of hate that's the hallmark of Othering. This is where despair is most deeply felt, for we realize that in spite of our advances to grow in self-worth and personal dignity, and build our lives, the gains can instantly be taken from us by people who are determined to oppress. While Chinh may have had some agency if he'd chosen to contact the police or confront the man, this wouldn't have changed the symbolic meaning of the man's attack. Racism is still as alive as it's ever been, and world events like the COVID-19 outbreak show that its hatred gets legitimized. With hatred so directed to China, Chinese people, and Asians who are mistaken for Chinese, Chinh suffered because he could not change the world.

If you've reencountered Otherness throughout your life, you're probably very clear on the sense of despair that comes with it. You may even feel ashamed if you let your guard down and came to believe that you wouldn't reencounter it. The healthier we grow—the more we move beyond the old, wounded messages that we're undeserving, immoral, criminal, sinful, or just plain wrong for being as we are—the more jarring hate feels when it's demonstrated in a primitive manner, like the man who spat on Chinh.

As you've read through this book, you've gained clarity about how rules of fear have shown up in your life. You're clear on how Otherness shows up and the many forms it takes. Our work now is to use the tools of change to keep you from sinking into despair when these things occur. For hate cannot be allowed to win.

The next section introduces a source of wonder that can deepen your work with all the tools of change. When we turn to nature and reconnect with the natural world, we embrace a powerful method for returning to our power as choicemakers. This can feel especially potent for those of us whose lives have separated us from the rhythms of our ancestral connection to the living planet.

Returning to Your Roots in the Natural World

Being in nature can unlock parts of yourself that have been dismissed and unvoiced. It is potent for your healing work, particularly when you experience despair. If you were raised in a culture that does not traditionally celebrate the land or recognize humanity as part of it, I realize this is an unfamiliar practice. But when you submit to the wonder of the natural world, you open the possibility for freedom from despair. This is a deeper promise from our earliest ancestors. We were born whole, and we need to now be reminded that wholeness existed before Otherness and despair ever did.

The Japanese description of taking in the sensations of the natural world is *shinrin-yoku,* or "forest bathing." Your forest bath can take place in any natural space that's accessible to you: the city park, a backyard, a desert trail, the shore. If you're a gardener, you already know the healing power of your natural space as you nurture beautiful plants and flowers into glory. Wherever you can experience the qualities of nature is where you need to be. Big or small, it doesn't matter.

When you enter these spaces, allow yourself to connect with gratitude for the spirit that guides you there. Having gratitude for the landscape is important. A few years ago, a couple from Maui taught me to ask trees for permission to enter their space. I was living in New England at the time, where the countless forest and seashore trails make it easy to remember to ask permission, by virtue of their wild beauty. Since moving to Chicago, I've continued to ask permission from the trees in our city parks to walk among them. Doing so resets my relationship with nature, reminding me that I'm the humble visitor and that it is an honor to enter such spaces.

Once there, allow your mind to simply observe the world around you. As the to-do lists and shoulds enter your mind—like "Oh, I should take a picture!" "I should ask so and so to do this with me!" "I really should go home and get things done"—label them "thinking" and simply be. Notice the natural space without giving in to the tendency to categorize it any ordered way like naming a type of bird or tree. Instead, simply observe them. Use your senses. Attending to the senses—what we see, hear, smell, touch, feel—tunes us into enduring elements of nature. Feel bark, leaves, soil, stone, and sand. Listen to soothing wind, laughing waters, or to the silence. Observe the creatures that dwell there. Move through with gratitude that such spaces exist.

Time in the natural world has a way of healing despair. It's hard to hold on to hurt when we open our hearts to awe. So seek out the freedom of a natural space, where you can notice the part of you needing this—silenced for too long, reeling from the prospect of all that might need to change in your life. Natural spaces also prepare us to use tools for change, beginning with clarity.

Weathering the Lows

As you read this chapter, you are likely considering the points in your life when you felt ready to give up and give in to the old, haunting messages that you are less than, an outsider, inferior. You've come far enough that you can recognize these points in time as distinct lows, versus existing in the constant state of believing you must be and act in a certain way to be tolerated. Still, the lows are there. When they show up, it seems like we're going to be feeling them forever. In such moments, we tend to confront every positive affirmation we know is true with "Yes, but..." and find some way to deny it—to stay stuck in Otherness and despair.

Our task is to gain skills for weathering the lows and recognizing them for what they are: transitory. It may seem hard to think of them as transitory when they feel so overwhelming. But the nature of feeling, both good and bad, is that it passes. Through it all, everything you experience and feel, there is a part of you untouched by anyone's judgment. This allows you to observe the present moment and its fundamental truth that you are whole just as you are, and not Other, even when you're hurting. This part of your healing journey does not minimize the pain you feel. Instead it recognizes that despair, while very real, is just one part of what you feel—it does not constitute what you fundamentally are. When you see despair this way, it does not define you any longer. It becomes just one part of the sum total that you feel and experience.

GAIN CLARITY ON THE TRANSITORY NATURE OF DESPAIR

To explore despair for your life without sinking into it, we're going to use the movie technique you learned in chapter 3. This will allow you to witness a moment of despair and see it clearly, along with the events that preceded and followed it. Once again, I suggest reading through the following instructions before beginning the exercise. Or you can listen to an audio recording that will guide you at http://www.newharbinger.com/46479. To prepare, focus on your breath to clear away distractions.

Allow your mind to drift to a moment in the past when you felt despair over being cast out as Other and then took specific actions that allowed you to heal. Maybe the circumstances that had you in despair changed, or maybe you changed your relationship with the circumstances. Focus on the moments when it seemed like mistreatment would never stop and you were feeling crushed by it. Holding that situation in mind, allow it to play in front of you like a sixty-second movie.

- For ten seconds, watch what your life was like at the time with all the things you had going on

- Spend five seconds watching the events that led up to your despair

- Devote five seconds to observing the despair you felt

- Give yourself forty seconds to witness what you did, said, thought, or realized that allowed you to heal from despair

Then allow the movie to end. If you're inclined, credits can roll with the names of anyone who was there for you and helped you through your despair. You can even include a player who Othered you, perhaps starring as the villain who's now gone. The closing score can be your power song. (Mine is "I Am What I Am"—I'm fond of covers by both Gloria Gaynor and Ginger Minj.)

Reflect on the movie and recognize that in moments when you experienced despair, the moment passed into history, and you arose. Perhaps you had people around you, maybe the help of a pet, who reminded you of your worth and helped pull you up. Or faith carried you. Or you found a great therapist. And you found the courage to be, choosing truth and freedom.

This activity can be used to reframe a lot of crises in your past. I use it in my own healing work to recognize the people and skills I had when surviving my father's suicide. It reminds me that if I lived through that hell, I can live through other things. This particular exercise can do so much, particularly when we're in a moment that we think we can't get through. Sometimes we need to recall our wisdom, strength, and resources—people, the natural world, institutions—to remind ourselves that we're more than the pain we're experiencing in this moment.

Self-compassion goes a long way toward healing despair too. Throughout this book, it's helped you address shame for past behaviors, old beliefs, and feelings accumulated over the years. We need compassion for ourselves because otherwise, as we realize any harm we were causing, it can slip into shame. As we wake up to thoughts like "Why did I give him so much power?!" we need an alternative response to shame. Similarly, self-compassion can address those times in our past when we were acting from the erroneous belief that *you cannot change the world.*

FORGIVE YOURSELF FOR ACTIONS
TAKEN IN DESPAIR

Moments of despair can lead us to disregard ourselves as well as others. Maybe we were angry and venomous to people because our despair was so deep. Perhaps we even harmed ourselves or attempted to do so. In this exercise, we identify these actions as products of despair, and begin the task of forgiving ourselves. Bring yourself into a state of mental rest and respond to these prompts in your journal.

Reflecting back on this chapter's clarity activity and other events from your life, can you see any patterns in your moments of despair? Consider the situations that seemed to bring them about, the physical, mental, emotional circumstances that led up to these moments of despair. What types of beliefs tend to swirl around in your brain? Look for similarities that exist across typical moments of despair.

Notice how despair played out for you. What did you sometimes do in response? Were you sarcastic and snappy, or did you isolate from people and not communicate? Did you get passive-aggressive and expect others to respond to hints that you needed to feel their love and reassurance? Did you turn your pain inward, while trying to appear normal and functional on the outside? Write down any things you did to your mind and body at those times. Did you abuse drugs, food, your finances, or your sexuality to harm others? Did you disrupt your health? Keep in mind this is not a time for judgment—you are simply becoming clear on your tendencies.

As you consider the times when you've despaired, choose a moment in particular that stands out to you right now. What do you think your older, wiser self—the one who's reading these words—needs to say to that younger self you were then? Because we're often more forgiving of others than we are of ourselves, it might be helpful to think of words you might say to someone you love when they acted from despair at a younger age. You can write this message as a formal letter or a series of statements in your journal.

Whatever form you choose, allow yourself to write from a place of acceptance for younger self, whoever they were and however they survived. What did that part of you need?

Showing compassion to ourselves for actions we've taken is sometimes challenging. We see the negative: the self-harm and the ways our actions impacted others. Being honest with ourselves allows us to get beyond judgement and recrimination. We didn't know what we didn't know. We knew of no other way to cope with despair than the methods available to us. For why would we? Part of being Othered was to be thrust into a barren landscape where survival was precarious. It's an emotional space of emptiness and futility.

Now we see Othering for what it is: someone else's lies—saying we are not equal to others, we are inferior and less deserving—that they attempted to instill in us. We now see how we took those lies and ran ourselves into the ground with them. We see the collateral damage we did to our own body and spirit, and perhaps the bodies and spirits of others. Here's Chinh's acceptance letter to himself.

> *Hey, Chinh! It's kind of weird to be writing to you—writing to myself. But here it is. Hey, I just want to say that I know you had it hard for a long time. Mom and Dad didn't really seem to want you. Maybe they cared in their own way, or they do now. But that doesn't matter so much anymore. It doesn't matter that you got so much bullshit from kids at school. Even now, people being racist can't send you into despair. Even the president being racist. It sucks bad, yeah. But it doesn't matter so much because it doesn't define you.*
>
> *You were in horrible pain. You were in agony. Nearly drinking yourself into a coma. Going along with assholes because you wanted their friendship. Being suspicious of the doctor who wanted to help when she saw you struggling in her class. You were just coping. You were hurting and you burned people or let them burn you. It was you being sad.*
>
> *You don't have to let this stuff sink you anymore. You don't have to be ashamed of how you acted. You're a more courageous person*

than that. You, a half-Asian kid who came to America after the war. Dude, nobody wanted Vietnamese people here! But you were here and you made it. Someday your life is going to be really cool! Your girlfriend's beautiful, smart, and together. You've got a lot of great friends around you. Your condo's nice too and Riblet's not even peeing on the rug anymore!

Finally, you'll have the life you deserve because of all the hard work you did. It's okay to be happy. You get to just be that, and never let others say that you're supposed to think less of yourself because you're Asian, or half-Asian, or whatever else they think. Who cares? You've got you! I've got me! Peace—Chinh

Like Chinh, we can see our way out of despair with clarity and self-compassion. We now have the power to forgive ourselves for despairing over others' lies, for buying the fear they peddled that we are unable to change the world. You understand that because you are a choicemaker who can choose where your energies go.

Now that you've seen your despair story, explored how you arrived at it, and given yourself compassionate wisdom for the process of healing, you'll use your creativity as a tool for addressing despair that may be happening now or that may arise in your future. You'll use sass to put this creative movement into action.

BRING TOGETHER CREATIVITY AND SASS TO CHOOSE A DIFFERENT PATH

Allow yourself to ease into a mindful state by tuning into your breath and the moment that exists now. Really notice the now, this instance in time. Feel the air in the room and the texture on the chair or sofa where you're sitting. Take in the sounds and other sensations that surround you.

Notice how it feels to be a resilient being who has walked this healing journey. Feel your strength and courage coming through to define yourself *for yourself.* Recall that every emotion is there to simply tell you what you need or don't need, and despair exists to call attention to what you're yearning for that feels lost. As you do, reflect on the following prompts and respond in your journal.

What is the single most valuable thing you rely on to move out of despair? This doesn't disrupt some other part of your life, instead it is your rock that restores solidity to your life when you're in despair. Is it your family or best friends? Is it a faith tradition? Perhaps it's the evolving planet and its tininess in the vast network of galaxies. Or the advancement of scientific inquiry through logical inference that helps us observe and understand. Whatever it is, bring this rock into focus.

If you've never had something you could recognize as a rock, try describing what that it might look like and consist of, if it were in your life. What resource do you wish you had or most want? Visualizing it will help move you toward having it in your life or discovering a resource that you hadn't thought of before now.

Give yourself time to bring this rock to the forefront of your conscious mind. What are the qualities that make it such a reliable resource in your life, now or in the future? Describe how it provides a foundation for your life, whether through words on paper, drawings with bold colors, lines in a meaningful pattern, images in a poem. This is about forming a powerful connection with the thing you can rely on most, so you have something solid to turn to when despair tries to sink you.

Whether you are developing your relationship to this resource rock or are deepening your understanding of it, allow your creativity to give you a method for understanding its function in your life. You can appreciate your rock anytime: before, during, and after moments of despair. This allows you to nurture it—the relationship, faith, mental faculty, hobby, intellectual pursuit, or however your rock is best described—during times when we are at our healthiest and most zestful. Now you just need the final tool, sass, to instigate activity and movement.

RESTORE SASS BY FINDING THE ROCK WHEN DESPAIR BEGINS

It's time to put plans into motion to keep you from sinking into despair. You'll be developing a Despair Plan for yourself. If you live in a place where frequent storms knock out the power, you're accustomed to keeping flashlights, candles, and extra batteries in an easily accessible place. A Despair Plan is no different. It puts resources at hand that help you deal with moments when you begin slipping into despair.

Your Despair Plan consists of clear and plainly written steps you will take when you find yourself in despair. To develop this, think about the rock you described in the previous exercise. What do you need to do to access this rock in moments when you need it most? With this question in mind, follow these instructions.

Establish the steps you will take when despair sets in. Something like, "I will resist the urge to try managing on my own, and just call my sister," "I will walk along the shore and talk to God," "I will recognize despair by the way it distorts truth, and interrogate it," "I will gaze up at the night sky and ponder its vast perspective." Just go with what works for you and break the process down into the steps you will take.

Choose something in your environment that offers a visual cue to remind you of your Despair Plan. It's an object you'll see every day that will act as an instant reminder of your plan, in case you need it. This can be an actual rock, a picture intentionally turned at an unusual angle, a symbol of your spirituality, whatever works for you. It just needs to be unusual enough so that, when you look at it, you remember why it's there. Keep this object handy.

Whenever despair shows up, follow the steps to access your rock. The first few times, test the plan and then modify it. Make it as practical and easy to use as possible. The important thing is that you have something in your immediate presence that breaks the train of despairing thoughts. The more you respond to despair with the active, thought-stopping process of your Despair Plan, the less severe and less frequent your experiences of Otherness despair will become.

As you leave this rule of fear behind, your final task is to live your truth. When you show up as you are, with all your colors and your magic, it is changing the world. As you begin freeing yourself from the responsibility of carrying other people's pain and brokenness, you give yourself permission to live as you wish, creating the story that you choose. Authenticity is beautiful. Through self-acceptance and love of our own spirit—no longer apologizing for taking up space—we do change the world. If others want to join us in this, then we will have found the people we really want and need for our lives.

As we move through our lives with a willingness to examine feelings of despair and address them directly when they start to sink us, we gain the ability to know our signs and signals. We may still fall into a pattern of despair, but when we do we will have tools and know what to do to address it. As we continue along our path, becoming progressively stronger, wiser, and more willing to be mindful, despair will feel more foreign. We recognize it as a more distant experience, something we had before, and might have again, but that tends to show up less frequently. In other words, things that once bothered us, that made us feel small and unworthy, no longer affect us as they once did.

This doesn't mean we're completely inoculated from stress, anxiety, grief, or crises in our lives. It certainly doesn't mean we'll shrug off incidents clearly aimed to demoralize or trivialize. It does mean we'll have a new system in place, with proven tools, for dealing with the internal shaming and self-hating that were once our go-to responses. We'll approach these experiences from a place of health, responding with pride and resiliency—from an understanding that we *are* whole, and always were, despite the narratives that once made us Other.

PART 3

LIVE FREE OF SOMEONE ELSE'S DEFINITION

CHAPTER 9

Weaken the Internal Oppressor's Stranglehold on Your Voice

It feels good to heal from damaging messages that you are "less than." As this happens, you strengthen the voice that says, "You are so much better than this mess you were handed." You become better at recognizing your boundaries and gain the ability to say "No." You stop ignoring emotional pain and instead ask, "What's this feeling about and what do I need to do with it?" The rules of fear begin to weaken, little by little, and you recognize that an oppressive world that harms, persecutes, and punishes does not take your self-worth with it.

That's a tall order, particularly when your Otherness story is stoked by legitimate fear for the safety of yourself and people you love. The stains of hatred will not be erased simply because we're becoming healthier and more whole. Yet, even as we mourn the dead and seek to advance peace and justice for those who are living, we must continue to work hard so despair does not win the day. In the last chapter, we looked deep into the sources of Otherness despair and identified ways to address them. Now we'll explore how to continue soaring freely, in spite of forces in life that can try us, and even break us, if we're caught without tools for dealing with them. Whether or not these life events are directly related to our Otherness, we can continue rising in spite of their unpredictability.

The COVID-19 virus pandemic taught us a lot about unpredictability. If there's one thing we learned, it's that life as we know it can change in an instant. Although the virus doesn't discriminate against Other people, its impact was magnified among communities of color and in poor neighborhoods—one and the same in many parts of America. Perhaps you got sick, lost someone dear, or experienced significant financial loss. On top of whatever happened, we were all isolated from resources: people we love, social outings, and routines that help us cope with stress like going to the gym. Like all of us, you probably experienced more than your share of worry, fear, hopelessness, and other painful reactions to the uncertainty of the times.

A lot happens over the course of our lifespans, and while the COVID-19 outbreak was a major event, there will be more crises to come. Whether we're grieving a loss, navigating global and personal disasters, or experiencing stress over finances, it can all make us feel alone and isolated. In our hearts and minds, being isolated bears a striking resemblance to feeling cast out. While the oppressive forces may be different from those that structurally Othered us in the past, life itself can feel like the oppressor. When we experienced life as oppressive, it cycles us back into feeling Othered.

Isolation is the main culprit that keeps our experience of being Other alive. Our task is to create ways to prevent isolation from taking hold of our heads and feeding our story of Otherness. Being able to stop mind-chatter before it takes us down shame's spiral is key to lifelong healing from Otherness. With all the twisted forms of social mistreatment you have endured—the barbs and terrible lies that somebody in a position of power and influence would have you believe about your worth—I suspect that nothing they said was as terrible as the things you've told yourself when you were in the pits of your own hell.

If we can recognize this tendency to sink ourselves, we can do some preventative work to keep it from happening. Our prevention efforts must begin with a commitment to refuse to give our self-esteem and sense of worth to people or systems that diminished us in the past. The people who cast us as Other, and the system they represent, must no longer be the compass point we follow.

We can learn to pick ourselves back up. A strong and unexpected headwind—whether a pandemic or a job loss or the death of a loved one—might knock us over and reinvoke that tendency to say to ourselves, "Well who do you think you are, anyway? You're just a _____." We may get hit with these things from time to time, but we don't need to stay down. It's important to recognize all the ways we still carry our oppressor's voice within us, making it our own and then reusing it against ourselves when life problems occur.

I think of this an internal oppressor: a voice that uses our moments of weakness to keep the shame cycle going. Although oppression and hate began outside of us, the internal oppressor was born long ago in school-yards, neighborhood streets, childhood homes, and landscapes where ancestors experienced extreme oppression. Sometimes direct, sometimes subtle, our internal oppressor uses an arsenal of weapons to demoralize us and keep us feeling subservient to the system of dominance that we've lived under. An internal oppressor doesn't need much to be sustained—it only needs negative self-talk and harsh critiques of who and how we are.

To weaken the internal oppressor, we must first understand its makeup, what it thrives on, and how it's reactivated in times of stress and exhaustion. With that in mind, let's delve into how internal oppression is fed and grows, and the thoughts it uses against us.

Understanding the Internal Oppressor

Healthy people who've done a lot of healing work still experience self-doubt, insecurities, depressed moods, and moments of heightened anxiety. In chapter 1, I shared the story of Jeanette, an African American humanities professor who felt that the world was always waiting for her to mess up. Here is more about her healing journey.

> Jeanette did a lot of personal-growth work over the years. She left the toxic academic environment that demoralized her and trivialized her contributions for another university where the leadership supported her research agenda and was genuinely excited about her work. Jeanette addressed Otherness trauma from her experience, including guilt for leaving students, grief for the time she spent believing her work held less merit, anger that she thought the problems in the racist and sexist department were hers to fix, and regret about bringing work stressors home. She forgave herself for being a less-than-perfect wife and mom.

Jeanette also took Otherness work into multiple areas of her life. She used it to navigate the complexities of a racist world as an African-American woman married to Danny, a Navajo man; raise multiracial children, including Danny's niece who had Down syndrome; her tendency to fall into supermom, super-daughter, super-professor roles; and all the exhaustion and disillusionment that resulted.

Years into her healing work, well after she understood "I am enough" and found freedom from the oppressor within, the COVID-19 pandemic hit. The first loss was her father, who was infected at a nursing home. Within three weeks, she lost a sister-in-law and an aunt, and had to attend their funerals virtually. As grief-stricken as she was, and as worried as she and Danny were for their family and extended network of relatives and close friends, Jeanette persevered. She worked to maintain a sense of normalcy and to contribute by making food deliveries to homebound neighbors, sewing masks, and trying to save the semester for her students.

Then Ahmaud Arbery, a Black man on a jog, was shot dead and she could no longer cope. When George Floyd died after a police officer kneeled on his neck for more than eight minutes, she was pushed further into despair. Jeanette's deep fear for the safety of all Black men, including her own sons, surfaced with intensity. While this fear was always with her, the rapid succession of violent deaths magnified it. They happened during a time of stress and isolation, when she could not connect with her extended family and friends.

Jeanette relived the trauma of being Othered and the sorrow passed down from her ancestors. She felt Danny's ancestral sorrow too. The result was sleepless nights filled with racing thoughts, and when she finally slept, she had disturbing dreams. She became so anxious about her grown sons' lives that she had to keep tabs on their movements just to keep going. Jeanette became weepier and more agitated, trying to eat instead of feel and shopping online to keep her mind occupied. Knowing that Danny was also worried for their sons, grieving the loss of his sister, and concerned about vulnerable family members he couldn't travel to check on, Jeanette didn't want to burden him. She felt alone and afraid. The feeling of being physically trapped was overwhelming: helpless to save the people she loved and unable to do anything about her stress and worry.

Like Jeanette, you're doing the work to heal Otherness. You're getting past the old messages of shame, being "less than," and constantly proving your worth to the world. Just as Jeanette's hard work has led her to make empowered life decisions, you too have grown stronger. Then you are faced with calamity, or even a series of them, and you feel knocked down and knocked out—just like times of old.

The "just like times of old" part is the one we really need to watch, for this is your internal oppressor trying to reassert control over your life. These questions can help you see how this happens and identify patterns that cause the internal oppressor to surface. Write the responses in your journal.

- What current world events make you feel most isolated or helpless?

- Is there an area of your life that you are grieving, whether losing someone to death, experiencing personal illness or a health decline, or ending a job or relationship?

- Is there a particular time of year—an anniversary, holiday, start of a season—that seems to cause memories of Othering experiences to surface?

- Are there significant financial worries, like an expensive repair on your car, a leaky roof, credit card debt?

- Do a family member's actions and choices create extreme stress for you?

- Are there stressors in your life at work, school, your spiritual home, or your community?

When you look over your answers, they may not seem directly related to your Otherness story. Take a closer look, and you may find that your experiences of Otherness and the isolation you feel are somehow awakened by these events. Isolation is the key issue here, as it is the hallmark of Otherness. In your journal, write down all the following statements that apply to you.

- When I have a problem, I prefer not to bother anyone with it.

- I have a tendency to bottle things up, in general.

- I'm silent a lot, even when I wish I could be heard.

- When I am stressed, I tend to do things alone.

- I spend a lot more time worrying about the future than people realize.

- I spend a lot more time regretting past mistakes than people realize.

Look over your responses and pay attention to how much time you spend alone and afraid. This short list can reveal how you may isolate in life during times when isolation is the last thing you need.

Of all the ways that a bully, dismissive teacher, disinvested caregiver, or any person tried to convince you of being "less than," you'll see that this oppressive person most effectively Othered you by using isolation to make you feel alone and afraid. Years later, long after these bullies may have disappeared from your life, your internal oppressor has you isolating again. That old messenger from the past is now an internal voice in your thoughts, and isolation is your go-to response for all life's stresses, hurts, and worries. You are convinced that you cannot bring important issues in your life out of isolation to seek help from people who care about you.

Otherness reasserts itself each and every time we self-isolate in our pain. It does so through our internal oppressor, who tells us that we shouldn't bother folks, we'll be okay, we just need to get our mind on other stuff. These are the messages that arise from the belief that we do not matter enough to represent who we are and what we need. Notice this within you for a moment.

Okay, it was a moment, and it has passed. You don't need to do this anymore.

We are now going to weaken this internal oppressor who has kept you alone and isolated as you deal with life problems. It may seem abstract to imagine life with a significantly weakened internal oppressor who doesn't get first say about you and your way of being. So we'll explore how this can look, and identify signs that the oppressor's hold on you is weakening.

Releasing the Stranglehold

As we heal from Otherness trauma, a number of notable changes occur. We start to think and act differently, in ways that at first are subtle. Maybe we don't sink as far when we overhear or see something that would have once demoralized us. If we do start to sink, we revisit our tools of change with a specific intent. Perhaps we spend a few minutes meditatively breathing and then talk back internally, saying, "Wait a minute—this mess isn't about me, and I'm not being gaslit into believing it is." We might refuse to rescue the self-esteem of someone who represents dominance in our lives, even becoming less interested in them or refusing to engage their games. If we must deal with them, we start representing ourselves as equals, worthy of having voice and space at the same table.

Each time we refuse to accept Otherness or someone's attempts to dominate and define us, we weaken our internal oppressor. These are actions that represent a change in beliefs about our worth, our right to be, our dignity. Every now and again, as we start practicing an approach to life that comes from strength and choicemaking, we recognize: "Oh yeah, I wouldn't have been able to do this before." That voice is what reveals how much you are changing and growing stronger. Here's what Jeanette did.

Jeanette felt anxious and worried, but then she realized what was happening. While crying alone in her kitchen one morning after Danny left for work, Jeanette recognized how similar these feelings of being alone and helpless were to what she felt back in middle school when the history teacher showed the class Gone with the Wind.

She spent the next several days piecing together the story. She had isolated in response to racism at the school she attended. Whenever she encountered stereotyped Black representation in films during her adolescence and young adult years, she had to hide her feelings. Many messages fed her sense that most could not see and accept her for who she is, from the limited choices of cosmetic products for her skin tone, to battling imposter syndrome in college, to being cast as an "angry Black woman" at her previous university. Her parents had attempted to assimilate, but Jeanette could see wisdom in the way her grandparents surrounded themselves with Black culture. Jeanette recognized that the isolation she was enforcing on herself was part and parcel of her story of being cast as Other.

With that realization, she determined to do things differently. She discussed her feelings with Danny and they talked frankly about the stress she'd been feeling and how worry was affecting her. He listened and allowed her to be as vulnerable as she needed to be. Then Jeanette reached out to a circle of women friends through a group chat and shared her experience—inviting them to be as candid. They responded with enthusiasm and relief, and the group chat helped them all navigate the intensity of the nationwide Black Lives Matter protests. With the support of her husband and close friends, Jeanette reached out to other faculty and the Black Student Union to organize a symposium at the university on antiracism. This led to a series of joint colloquia with other campus groups who were also addressing race and cultural disparities for Latinx, Asian, and Native American and First Nations Peoples.

As she reoriented the compass of her life so she was directed by a sense of agency, Jeanette felt purposeful and mobile. It didn't make her grief over the deaths disappear, nor did it alleviate her fear for her sons' safety. But with channels open to connect and feel heard, make an impact, and create safe spaces for others to voice their experience, Jeanette was able to overcome despair's paralysis.

Jeanette made a conscious choice to not allow her internal oppressor to win. When she made a conscious choice to use her power, her voice, and her knowledge as a Black woman, wife, mother, professor, and loving friend, she found she could get through calamity without despair and make powerful choices for the future.

Similarly, even the most difficult and isolating of times, we must make the choice to become aware of our internal oppressor. As we do so, it's helpful to ask, "What is feeding my inner oppressor right now?" and "In what ways am I allowing myself to be isolated?" Once alert, we can combat these tendencies by reaching out to build community with people who are directly invested in us or share our concern.

We win by refusing to isolate. The internal oppressor you have draws on specific source material and knows how to use it against you. So does mine. Oh, our stories are quite different. Our reference points, our cultures, our languages, and even how we take in and process information likely differ. Yours may have been centuries in the making. But just as you get into your headspace and start feeling alone and afraid, so do I, so does Jeanette, so do many of us who've been cast as Other. In spite of all the years each of us has spent believing we're the only one who retreats into isolation, *we are not alone.* As scary as it is, it is restorative to find spaces where we can be vulnerable and real, together, about the things that were previously isolating us.

Our internal oppressor will try to rekindle each rule of fear that has silenced and oppressed us in the past. We have the right of refusal. So we can say "Yes" to many new things. We say *yes!* to being heard by someone who loves us, who wants to feel needed by us. We say *yes!* to our right to share voice and a perspective others need to hear. We say *yes!* to inspiring people's courage through our example. We say *yes!* to all the zest that comes with finally allowing ourselves to take up the space that's ours to fill.

We must learn to live our truth, defined by neither external oppressors nor their messages that we internalized and made our own. To do this, we redefine our space in the world and how we represent it within, and between, our roles in life. We get to determine how we want to show up as individuals, partners, parents, professionals, creators, influencers—all the roles we occupy. This really is our moment in history.

As we become less referential to our oppressors as the source of how we believe we're supposed to be and act, a natural question arises. We ask, "Who am I, if not that?" To truly define yourself—for no one but yourself, without someone else defining how you are supposed to think, live, and feel—you have a lot of exploring to do.

GET CLEAR ON WHAT TO REFUSE AND WHAT NEEDS A YES

To help answer this question, we'll use the clarity tool. Once again, read through the full set of instructions before beginning the practice. You can use breathwork, with a lowered gaze and focused concentration on your breath. Or you can simply observe the moment, perhaps paying attention to a physical feature like your hands or legs. Music or quiet, a gentle walk or absolute stillness—do whatever works for you to clear your mind. It will be what's right for this moment.

Focus on the internal oppressor, who may still lurk in the shadows. It may help to personify this as a mental picture of yourself at a fragile moment when you lack confidence and are acutely feeling the deepest hurts of Otherness. Or maybe a mental snapshot arises of an actual oppressor from your life or someone who represents the word "oppressor." Gain a sense of this part of you, noticing the kinds of messages used to weaken you. With this image in mind, follow these steps and record reflections in your journal.

1. Become aware of the time windows when your internal oppressor shows up. Does it go to work on you at night, while you're at work, or during another period of the day?

2. Recall these words from a previous chapter: "What is fed will grow. What is starved will die." What types of experiences feed the internal oppressor? In other words, what situations in the outside world cause your internal oppressor to come out of the shadows and begin haunting you?

3. Considering the circumstances that cause your experience of Otherness to resurface in your present life, what do you need right now to prevent your internal oppressor from being fed?

4. You can starve it by saying "No." In what areas of your life do you need to say "No" to someone or something? Begin a flow of ideas and see where it leads you.

5. Saying "Yes" can either feed or starve your internal oppressor, so list as many yeses as you need in your life. Allow them to come to mind and write them down without edits or judgment. Let the ideas flow.

6. Consider your responses and choose what actions to take, when.

Weakening your internal oppressor is really about the direct actions you'll choose to take. When you reencounter things in your present life that remind you of the past times when you were cast out as Other, taking these actions will keep you from sinking back into old experiences of shame.

Healing Otherness is an ongoing effort. We continue to address new issues that arise while gaining skills for addressing old stuff that tends to revisit us. As we become clearer on what we will accept and what we choose to walk away from, we create the opportunity for real change to occur. When confronting the ignorance and hate that would have once plunged us back into feeling our worth diminished, we can now make choices to protect our emotional health.

A deep way to support emotional health is to find compassion for this internal oppressor. It may seem counterintuitive to hold compassion for the part of you that lingers in the corners, ready to pounce on moments of weakness. After all, didn't you just describe how you would starve this tendency of yours?

Yes, but consider this. By offering compassion to the parts where your darkest and most shaming thoughts about yourself have resided, you can live free from the cycle of Otherness. This makes sense if you think about how you've used compassion in previous chapters to forgive, love, and accept the things you did from states of hurt at earlier times in your life. Now, you're offering compassion to a part of you weakened by your work throughout this book. The internal oppressor is a part of your memory, so finding compassion for it releases its control over your life.

FIND COMPASSION FOR YOUR INNER OPPRESSOR

Allow yourself to reenter your mindful space. Really move into a state of existing in, and accepting, the present moment for what it is. Recognize the years of hurt, longing for love and approval, wanting to be visible and to matter. Then drift back to the image of your inner oppressor. See this part of you attempting to use your Otherness story against you, needing so much of your energy to do so. Imagine you internal oppressor sitting in front of you. See the wounds and all the unmet longings that it represents. As you see this part of you, consider the following questions and reflect on them in your journal.

- What do you need to say to this part of you in order to address its role in your life?

- Are there emotions, like anger, rage, or grief, about this part of yourself that need to be expressed?

- What has this part of you been trying to accomplish? Love, approval, status, safety? Become clear on your inner oppressor's goals and write them down by completing the sentence "I recognize you've tried to...."

- In spite of this part of you, what were you able to do, perhaps in unexpected ways? Describe your defiance for the internal oppressor to understand.

- When your internal oppressor attempts to revisit you in the future and reassert control over your belief about yourself, your actions, and your feelings, how will you respond compassionately? Imagine what you will say and do, explaining to the internal oppressor in detail.

Compassionately understanding your inner oppressor is a deep cleanse that allows you to be free of the destructive tendency to think and act from a place of Otherness. It may be one of the most complex and powerful forms of healing we can do. Holding ourselves with compassion for all the stuff we did in fear, and accepting how we coped in the past, makes it possible to offer compassionate understanding to a variety of life experiences that come our way.

Embracing every part of ourselves, especially the parts that existed in the deepest realms of shame, frees up an extraordinary amount of mental space. It can be startling to discover how much space we've given to negative thoughts about ourselves, and how much they controlled our actions—in many areas of our lives. As you practice compassionately understanding all the parts you were ashamed of within yourself, you'll be more loving toward yourself in general.

Freeing yourself from this type of shame allows you to see more of what you want from life, and to perceive those desires without judgment. This is when you enter a process of creation. So let's create a personal judgment-free zone.

You may already be a very loving and accepting person who's not especially judgmental of others. You might be the kind of friend and ally who also very consciously creates safe spaces and judgment-free zones for people who've been cast out as Other—offering kindness, empathy, advocacy, emotional energy. But how often have you considered creating a zone that's free from you judging yourself?

Our work in this chapter wouldn't be complete if we didn't engage in creating a personal judgment-free zone for yourself. After all, having moved beyond the need for an internal oppressor, it's now time to specify the *yes!* that you need to give yourself. This is the promise of moving past all the muck of your past and the tendency to tell yourself to say "No" to things you vitally need and deserve in order to be fulfilled. Here's what Jeanette created for herself.

Jeanette identified a flower bed in her backyard as her judgment-free zone. This was the place where she'd experiment and be allowed to make mistakes, trying new plants and landscaping ideas rather than relying on the "tried and true" beds in more visible parts of her yard. She decided to decorate her judgment-free zone with various sources of inspiration: a verse from the Bible on a garden stone, a reflecting globe, some painted metal figurines, and hand-painted signs with cheerful sayings. She grouped her plantings in a wave-like design to lend a sense of motion and free movement. It soon became her favorite part of the yard.

Like Jeanette, you have the ability to create a space that represents your truth. Offer this to yourself with no judgment. Make a place to be that brings you joy.

CREATE YOUR PERSONAL JUDGMENT-FREE ZONE

Begin with clearing your mental space through meditation, focus, or music. Allow yourself to notice the parts of you that still yearn for freedom from judgment, but you're still holding back. What's there that hasn't been acknowledged so far in your healing journey, and is now getting your attention? Consider what your personal judgment-free zone needs to include. Here are some things to keep in mind.

- This zone is a representation of what you want and need in your life, as you are going to live it, no longer bound and defined by Otherness and your oppressors.

- Your judgment-free zone is the place you get to enter where you accept *You* for the choices you wish to make, the feelings you have about life experiences, and the decisions you've made that brought you here.

- The zone is your own, and you specify the terms. You can state these terms to anyone who chooses to be in your life, in a manner of your choosing.

It's helpful to think of this judgment-free zone as a physical space, perhaps an area of your home, yard, or the park down the street. Is it an empty space where you explore new ideas or things about yourself? Visualize this and bring it to life. You can write out a physical description of how it looks. You can draw it, represent it as a vision board, maybe use a file in Pinterest. There's no one way to do it.

The beauty of your judgment-free zone is that you decide what you will keep, and what you'll shed as gently as the fur of an old collie. Choicemaking is a powerful activity. It allows us to claim a level of ownership in our lives that is unlike anything we've had before. Even before we had experiences that we now recognize as Othering, we were being instructed on who we needed to be and how, and were told how life was to be conducted. Maybe some of that has worked for you, or maybe very little has.

As you begin existing with intentional freedom—from the rules of fear that external oppression created and that internal oppression caused to linger— a great deal will shift in your life. You'll have the opportunities, and witness the life consequences, that come with choicemaking—and therefore possess a stronger ability to accept these terms and live with them. You'll also have more tools for addressing the pain of situations that arise—and they will—so you don't isolate as you did in the past. Importantly, the personal compass you reference to navigate will orient you through your own definitions of self and culture. No longer navigating by the rules of an external group, you can find your way home.

CHAPTER 10

Find Your Way Home Through Community

We have been through a lot together. You've done so much to be able to claim space in the world and refuse to be defined by the shadow of Otherness. Your conscious decisions have led you to a state no longer ruled by fear, which means your oppressors cannot determine beliefs you have about yourself. This work allows you to shape your life and identity around freedom by being a choicemaker. With the creation of space for *You* to occupy, you naturally pave the way for finding and building your place of belonging.

This chapter is about creating community in your life. If you already have a strong community of people who do not require you to deny or leave out parts of your life in order to have a place with them and who love and accept you as you are, your work in this chapter will help fortify and expand this place of belonging. If you're searching for a place of acceptance and are unsure where to begin, this work will help you define the search. We will use skills you've gained throughout this book to determine your next steps to be part of a community that helps you thrive.

As you've no doubt seen, growing healthier in life has often meant moving away from people who've harmed you. Perhaps you've entered community spaces that reflect your understanding of yourself today, only to find that not everyone who has been Othered in similar ways has dealt with their wounds and scars. It can be disheartening to go through so much change in your life, encountering so much discovery and drawing on such courage, and then encounter people in your new life who aren't on the same page. In some cases, you may have been surprised and disillusioned to find people who have overcome tremendous adversity—who were, in some ways, admirable and perhaps even heroic—but are none-theless quite toxic and on a very different path than you.

This toxicity can show up in very surprising ways. Perhaps you made bold decisions and showed up in a new spiritual community, only to find that instead of relating with your values of charity, compassion, enlight-enment, and family, you encountered divisiveness, gossip, greed, and other problematic qualities you had hoped to leave behind. Maybe you made a big move away from the place you grew up, hoping to get away from a climate that felt pessimistic, defeating, and very damaging to your spirit. But the people in your new area demonstrated a lot of the same characteristics you were trying to get away from, or they presented other problematic behaviors that you felt ill-equipped to address. Or you went to art school and encountered shady students and disengaged teachers. If you chose a new profession from a place of empowerment, you may still encounter toxic people. People do the same things you encountered in the past, leaving you feeling disappointed—if not deeply hurt.

This is a hard challenge. Even though people had Otherness experi-ences of their own, they are still accustomed to the power structures in place among the cultures in which they grew up. Though many of them put a lot of work into distancing themselves from their communities of origin, they sometimes recreate problematic power structures in which somebody is being cast out as Other. Jaime's story helps illustrate what it's like to step into such a community.

> Jaime was born to a small family of farmers in Veracruz, Mexico just before the North American Free Trade Agreement (NAFTA) was signed. By the time he was eight, American agribusiness had wiped out his family's ability to sustain their farm. The lack of available work forced the family to immigrate to America to avoid starvation, and his parents found employment at a midwestern slaughterhouse.
>
> Growing up in rural America, Jaime was Othered in many ways. Anti-immigration picketers at the slaughterhouse used derogatory language, hissing and yelling at the workers. At school, the immigrant children banded together and relied on each other. Jaime's feelings of

Otherness grew as he became fluent in English and understood the words of hate used against him, his parents, and his friends.

When Jaime was twenty years old, he moved to a large city where he came out as gay. The city represented both a physical and mental space of freedom for him and he was excited to start his new life. Yet, with as much promise as the new city held, it wasn't long before he began encountering forms of Otherness within the gay community. Bars seemed to segregate along racial lines, as well as lines dividing body size and shape.

Jaime was perplexed by the odd sense of unbelonging in gay bars. They seemed predominantly White and "A-gay" biased. Jaime was not affluent, fit, nor socially connected. As a brown-skinned person of Nahua ancestry, he alternated between feeling invisible—with no one speaking to him or seeming to even notice his presence—and occasionally being exoticized through questions like "So wow! What are you and, um, where are you from?"

The question "What are you?" was particularly isolating because it was something he'd asked himself for years as he contemplated his history, family's immigration and life in America, and his sexual identity. Online dating proved equally discouraging, as many men's profiles stated things like "No fats, no femmes, no Asians." This left him questioning his place among gay men, a world that seemed to shut so many people out.

Jaime's story reflects the rollercoaster experience of working hard to make life changes, only to find that new places we occupy can present barriers similar to those from our past. Encountering these things in new settings, where we should feel at home, seems to cut even more deeply. With all the courage and sacrifice we make to live our personal truth, we expect that somehow things will be different in a chosen community. Just as Jaime was disillusioned by racism, classism, femmephobia, and fatphobia within the gay male community, you may have been surprised to encounter barriers in new communities that you had expected to call home. After all, isn't the promise of overcoming the pain of being cast out as Other that you'll find a place of acceptance where you can lay down your burdens among a like-minded community of people who care about your struggle and are invested in not repeating it?

I contend that we must keep that promise alive as a light to guide our ship by, as we continue sailing past people and communities who are not invested in our needs. Acceptance is so very central to our well-being. Healing our stories, including ancestral stories, requires that we find people who can support our continued growth. Rather than remaining disillusioned when we don't first encounter this, it's essential that we continue the effort.

The Continuing Quest for Community

We work hard and make sacrifices to reclaim our mental spaces from oppressors, and are deliberately creating change in our lives. So we're not going to give up any of that space to a new set of oppressors simply because they show up in settings we claimed for ourselves. We must protect our mental well-being, regardless of who is Othering us and where it happens. You're showing up in new environments and claiming your right to be there. So what happens when the space isn't what you want and need?

You have the answer to this already. One skill being Othered taught you is perseverance. Finding community is one more life area where perseverance is needed. The logical question is "How?"—how do you find people who get you, who don't view you in transactional terms for what you can give them, who value your life contribution, and who don't require you to morph according to their expectations for you?

We need to define community for ourselves. We can talk about community as our neighborhood, town, or region. It can be a defining characteristic of our identity that's shared with others, as in the LGBTQ community or Deaf community. As people who have been Othered, we've deliberately chosen to show up in these communities. Yes, being born deaf may encourage you to identify with the Deaf community and Deaf culture, and at the same time you may want to join communities in a variety of life areas that also reflect kinship, shared values, and a sense of connection.

Each community we participate in, even the ones we're born into, reflects our choice to be there. We make a conscious decision to engage people who share an aspect of our lives through shared values. It's essential to recognize this choicemaking. For just as you've chosen to address the story of Otherness you were told, not allowing it to continue defeating messages about your worth as a human, you also must choose to be with people who support your worth.

First, we notice our relationships with the people we choose to call our community, identifying the qualities and textures of these relationships. Doing so will allow you to create and sustain more of what's necessary for your life so you can find love, safety, fulfillment, and whatever else you seek.

CLARIFY THE STRENGTHS IN YOUR COMMUNITY

Let's begin. Prepare yourself by gathering your notebook or journal. Read through the instructions before you start. Use the breathing exercise that's worked for you throughout the book. You can drop your gaze, close your eyes, follow the process of slow and deliberate breath, and allow yourself to simply *be*. Or you may rest your attention on a physical feature and simply notice its qualities and the physical sensations in this moment. Sit in silence, or with soft background music without distracting lyrics, and allow yourself to simply be. If you have interrupting thoughts, simply label them "thinking," and allow yourself to return to your breath, your focus on your hands, or however else you're tuning in. As you become fully aware and present, notice the following.

- In your life, who allows you to feel most understood?

- Which community in your life inspires you to be most vulnerable and free?

- How do these people make it clear that you're safe with them?

- What would their response be if you brought up something hurtful, regrettable, or humiliating?

- What are you doing to feed and honor these relationships in your life?

This process probably feels emotional in some way. Bringing to mind people we love, who also love us, tends to do that. You may have found there are people you're close to, but have struggled to let in. The scars of our Othering run deep, and while we're pretty good at taking care of other people, we often construct big defenses. Or we have invested in creating an image of being invincible, and we're frightened to admit the truth to others. Seeing the ways people do support us, and also the ways we limit them, help us choose community.

The questions you answered will help you begin recognizing what you can expect in *growth-fostering relationships* (Miller and Stiver 1997). This is a really important concept! We can do great work to heal through meditation, reflection, art, and music—dismantling the destructive tendencies in our lives that were seeded on the day we were cast out as Other. Yet, without being connected to people who allow us to be authentic and can appreciate our quirks, ways of expression, or deep belly laughs, we cannot truly be free. As a tribal species, we depend on people who make us feel loved, safe, and accepted just as we are. These relationships are building blocks for mental health, and we can see how this would be true as we recover from the damage inflicted in being Othered. For in all of the experiences you had of being cast out, you deserve to now be embraced for the freedom you have claimed.

In the course of our healing journey, we find ourselves needing change. Our community may not offer what we need, and we may realize that we don't have relationships in place to offer support and allow us to expand and grow.

Your Changes, Reflected in Community

If you find that your community is lacking in some way, you're not alone. The process of making a conscious choice to continue healing from Otherness involves moving away from people who bring toxicity to your life—whether through mind games and manipulation, power struggles that leave you feeling the need to constantly defend yourself, or attacks on your self-esteem that exhaust you. The relationships that make you most unhappy in your life are likely the ones where someone is using your history of Otherness against you. Say you're a woman who was Othered for her body size or shape. Chances are that, even as you healed, the relationships that remain the most hurtful use body-shaming when the someone wants to inflict hurt. People who are willing to use our deepest hurts against us are not well.

Sadly, exposure to these types of relationships can leave you feeling that no one is safe, and that you cannot trust anyone. Remember all the talk about isolation in the last chapter? It supports the internal oppressor. When you've learned to move away from toxic people, then made a bold choice to put yourself out there again and taken a risk to do it—only to encounter toxic people at first—it's normal to initially retreat into isolation. "Initially" is the keyword here, because we need to continue showing up.

As we venture into new communities, we do need to be alert. We may encounter people who sense our newness and the vulnerability it entails. They can try to take advantage of us as they sense our eagerness to connect, or perhaps our naivety about the group's cultural norms. Alcoholics and Narcotics Anonymous groups deal with something called "13th-Stepping," in which an experienced member pursues romantic involvement with someone new to recovery. The new person is vulnerable, still adapting to sobriety, and can be seduced by wisdom and support from a person who's been sober for a long period of time. The phenomenon can apply to all kinds of communities.

It is exploitative, for the new person who's just made the brave decision to join has done so with the expectation that the power of group will be a source of change. When such an imbalanced and exploitative relationship becomes toxic, as it often does for people in vulnerable states, the chance for relapse—whether into substance abuse or isolation—is significant. Seeking out a community of healing, being exploited in it, perhaps assuming the shame and responsibility for what went wrong, and then isolating back into our struggle, can become a cycle. This happens in many ways as we choose bold and radical new lives for ourselves. The vultures are circling.

Other times, the members of a group just ignore you and you struggle to make connections. We showed up, determined that this was going to be our thing. Then the people we hoped to meet and forge community with were not there. We tried, showed up, and even brought a humming-bird cake. But they could not be bothered. In these instances, the well-worn path leads us back into isolation, the home of our internal oppressor who's ready to shame the hell out of us for trying to venture out.

Through all these experiences of movement and change, of trying to connect with people and forge community, we learn more about ourselves and what we really need to feel in order to experience community. For simply having a shared characteristic with people, whether our race, sexual identity, or other aspect is only a start. It is usually not enough to find connection. You're a complex intersectional being. Your life story joins together many aspects of self: gendered, racial, sexual, cultural, phys-ical, intellectual ways of being. You play many life roles that might include partner, parent, professional, social organizer or quiet friend. This includes being a lover of music, gardening, or cheesemaking, and the things you like to do on a Sunday afternoon. Jaime found that while gayness was a sense of identification and orientation, many other aspects of his life were equally important and needed to be not only seen, but honored.

While working in a print shop, Jaime discovered a love of graphic design. As he pursued his interest, he found a community of creative people: tattoo artists, muralists, sculptors, and a larger group of their partners, spouses, and friends of the arts. They were invested in each other's work and the practice of creativity. This community was a mix of people also drawn to urban life, and they helped Jaime discover new forms of music, philosophy, and other things that came to matter to him. They were from various regions and had different cultural backgrounds, gender and sexual identities, ways of thinking and being. This community of creativity expanded Jaime's language for gender identity, and Jaime began identifying as gender-queer and using the pronoun "they."

Equally, Jaime had an impact on the people around them, producing art that signaled life as a Mexican immigrant with ancestral roots in the original peoples of the Americas. Their art became bolder and more confident, supported by a community who cared about Jaime's story and their right to be, in all their identities—queer, Mexican, artist, vegan, lover of people and freedom.

Like Jaime, you have a variety of parts of self—some reflecting areas where you've been Othered and some where you've been included. All these parts of you may be enriched by a community of people who share an aspect of your life or happily celebrate it in you. To help you identify new areas where you may need to forge community, we'll turn once again to the clarity tool.

CLARIFY WHAT YOU NEED FROM COMMUNITY

Prepare yourself for this mindfulness activity by focusing your attention on the breath, one of your physical features, or another object. Allow mind-chatter about to-do lists or other preoccupations to release. Spend some time deepening your process, being in the moment and allowing yourself to flow with it. When you are ready, consider the following and reflect in your journal.

- Is there an important aspect of your identity that you're not able to express in your present community—but are yearning to? Consider your race, culture, sexuality, language, gender, spirituality, where you're from, where you live now, and your ways of thinking and doing.

- What is the area of your life where you feel most like an outsider right now, where you wish you weren't? Is it a role you play in community, parenting style, political position, interest, hobby, or form of personal expression? Allow yourself to notice your yearning for connections that you don't yet have.

- What additional community needs do you have right now? Do you need a space where you can be playful and laugh without fear of judgment, or be with people who don't require you to rescue them? Maybe you need a group to share a form of recreation. Notice this need and name it: "I need people who...."

Observing your life in this way may lead you to realize where you feel unseen. Perhaps this has been bothering you for some time, or maybe you're only now becoming aware of it. You're yearning to be seen and recognized, to feel the energy of a community of people who seem to say, "We recognize this part of you. We celebrate it. You have an impact on us." In order to arrive there, it's essential that you're also willing to see this part of you.

This is often such a challenge when we've been Othered. Experiences of rejection taught us that in order to be in a community, we must leave significant parts of ourselves out. This takes us back to the rule of fear from chapter 5, which insists that we must tone down our differences. Even as we heal from this rule and the losses it brought, we must acknowledge that these parts of us need to be seen. It takes courage and self-acceptance to find a community that also accepts us.

Jaime's story shows the impact that community had. Through exploring music, art, lifestyle, and even definitions of self and gender, Jaime grew. Their own experiences of Mexican heritage—rich with language, culture, and ways of being—integrated into their story as a gay gender-queer person. Jaime created an intentional space in an affirming community, where relationships allowed each other to see, be seen, and have impact, within which they could all be positively impacted through mutual exchange.

Learning to take up space in the world, without needing to apologize, comes with an important commitment to also offering accepting space for others. As we form community in our lives, it's crucial to foster inclusion for people around us who've also been Othered and now need to be seen. In doing so, we begin to dismantle Otherness within our community. To bring this home, we'll engage the compassion tool.

Compassionately Reflecting on People

So far in this book, we've used compassion to deliberately forgive parts of our history where we felt shame and regret. We have allowed compassion to play a central role in acknowledging the places we've been in our lives—all of which led us to this moment. Now we're going to expand compassion beyond the self, allowing its influence to permeate our community and reach beyond it.

This is an expanding ethic that builds upon our own healing work. What important work it is! Had we shifted focus to the needs of people around us before doing the necessary healing work in our own lives, we may have continued the trend of caretaking people around us without acknowledging our own needs and struggles. But you have done that work. Having engaged the journey to free yourself from damaging beliefs that Otherness instilled, you're ready to practice compassion for those around you.

I view compassion work as an advanced step in healing. After all, if there's anything a story of Otherness has taught you, it's that you are not alone. Your oppressors wanted you to think you were—for as long as you held these beliefs, your diminished state could serve them. You are not colluding with your oppressor's lies anymore. Nor are you going to recreate oppression in someone else's life. Instead, you will cultivate compassion for all people's Otherness experiences.

This compassion exercise has four parts that build on each other. I suggest becoming comfortable with one before moving on to the next. Doing this level of compassion-giving work can feel exhausting and overwhelming, so please don't rush into giving more than you comfortably can, and make that a practice. It's important to respect yourself and your limits, honoring the strength and the giving ability you have in this moment. At the same time, do push yourself to expand feelings of compassion for the Other. You can listen to audio recordings of all four parts of this exercise at http://www.newharbinger.com/46479.

To prepare for each of these activities, use your preferred mindfulness method and find a state of stillness. Focus on your breath, your hands, or whatever allows you to singularly focus. Clear your mind and follow these prompts.

EXPAND COMPASSION FOR THE OTHERNESS
OF SOMEONE YOU LOVE

Notice all the compassion you've given to yourself recently. In particular, notice how much compassion work you've done over the course of this book as you addressed each rule of fear. Observe how compassion feels, with its qualities of love, forgiveness, understanding, and acceptance.

Visualize compassion as a light that exists in the center of your chest. It emanates throughout your body, all the way to your extremities. Feel the sensations, the power of your choice to heal, and the freedom that comes with it.

As you continue doing this, think about someone who's close to you who has been Othered. Focus on that person. Notice their story of Otherness as you understand it, recalling all the fear instilled in them and all the hurt you've witnessed. As you do this, breathe in that fear and that story of Otherness. Breathe out your compassion, your light. Allow all the love you've learned to give yourself to now be shared with this person.

Continue to breathe in their suffering and breathe out your compassion. With each breath, see the light of your compassion grow stronger, expanding to surround this person. Allow compassion to continue growing. Spend five minutes or so focusing on compassion for the suffering this person feels. Then slowly transition out of the visualization. Afterward, describe whatever thoughts and feelings arose during the practice in your journal.

Deliberately sharing compassion for another person who has been Othered shifts the nature of our relationship with them. As you grow in the practice of giving compassion in this very deliberate way, it becomes the first thing you think about when you bring the person to mind.

We naturally carry compassion for people we love. By continuing this practice of breathing with compassion, for this individual and perhaps others in your immediate community circle, you build your own well of self-compassion and your ability to give it with deliberate effort.

As you become more accustomed to this practice, you can extend compassion beyond your immediate circle. If at any point the work feels overwhelming, simply return to your own breath and allow the light of compassion to reside within you. Your practice of giving compassion really depends on feeling centered, clear, and in a balanced state. Forcing yourself to give compassion when you're depleted may lead you to resent someone, which hooks you back into the rule addressed in chapter 6—that you must work twice as hard. That's not needed. Do this from a place of joy and love.

FOSTER COMPASSION FOR OTHERNESS IN YOUR COMMUNITY

Return to a quiet mind and find your place of compassion, allowing its energy to emanate from the center of your chest into the rest of your body. Continue breathing with compassion, allowing it to strengthen and grow in intensity.

As you do, see the people in your community—perhaps one based on physical location or a cultural connection. Bring them into focus. See the Otherness stories they have carried: some may be like your own and some will be different. Witness their stories, their oppression, their fears. Bring faces to mind and breathe in their collective stories of Otherness. Breathe out with compassion. Allow your compassion to grow with each exhale, emanating to each person and corner of your community.

Continue your breathing. Now see the Otherness stories you are aware of in communities near you or that have also been Othered. Breathe in the stories, the fears, the suffering. Breathe out your compassionate light, witnessing them as you give compassion to their Otherness. Allow your compassion to continue expanding to larger and larger groups of people— eventually reaching communities with Otherness stories that you don't know much about. See your compassion washing over them, being felt in all corners of their experience, the lives of their children, and the hearts of everyone they contact.

FEEL COMPASSION FOR THE OTHERNESS OF ANCESTORS

Visualize a previous generation of people being Othered. Allow yourself to witness their stories, their fears, their hurt. Breathe in these stories, and exhale compassion. Let the light of your compassion grow stronger with each exhale. Continue on, keeping in mind the previous generation and then a generation from the century before them. Progress through history and follow the practice. Bring a generation to mind. Witness their collective story of Otherness through enslavement, forced famine, genocide. Breathe out compassion for their suffering, allowing its light to become part of history, as you move deeper and deeper into the tribes of humans—as far as your mind can reach into our ancestral history.

Allow yourself to grow stronger with each offering and let compassion grow within you each time you breathe. Witness them, honor them, and let their Otherness stories become part of your own wisdom now, so you can be a source of change for their descendants.

FIND COMPASSION FOR AN INDIVIDUAL YOU HAVE OTHERED

As a final exercise, at a time when you are ready, bring your compassionate focus to anyone you may have Othered in the past or may be Othering now. Witness their story of Otherness and your role in it. Feel the compassion you now have for yourself, and extend that compassion to them. Continue to breathe in their Otherness and breathe out compassion. Spend as much time as you need to allow the compassionate understanding of this person's Otherness to become clear. Allow yourself to see what you did not see before.

Offering compassion in such deliberate ways allows us to make radical shifts in our lives. We begin to create community in a wholly different way, refusing to give in to Othering or accept it as a natural state of affairs. Instead, we can approach relationships from our lens of clarity, compassion, creativity, and sass. As we do, we bring our awareness to others' experiences, perhaps committing that our presence in community will offer them safety, change, and joy.

This doesn't mean we become rescuers and caretakers for people who are capable of doing things for themselves. Nor does it mean that we start neglecting our needs again. But it does mean that we refuse Otherness as a continual way of being. We refuse to use Otherness to block people's entry into spaces of equity and inclusion. As I said before, we are all equal. Fostering community is a celebration of this.

Writing this book for you has been a source of change in my life, and I sure hope reading it has had a similar effect. To say, "These are uncertain times," feels cliché—for when is this not true? Uncertainty and change are ways of life, because nothing remains static. This doesn't have to be scary. The story of Otherness has taught us that change needs to happen—and you and I get to be that change. We don't have to exist pinned under the rules of fear that were imposed by our story of Otherness. Nor do we have to slip back into old patterns of negative self-talk when new experiences come our way. Instead, we get to be deliberate change agents in our communities.

You can have so much clarity, compassion, creativity, and sass that you live very intentionally in ways that work for you. Jaime's story showed how, when you own your rights as a choicemaker, you can choose to live free. Freedom leads to building community among people who respond to your expressions of freedom and to the compassion you demonstrate.

With that said, be powerful. Be loving to yourself. Be compassionate to every being on this planet of ours, including those here before us. You have worked hard and earned your right to be here. You always deserved a place at the table, and now you're claiming it.

Welcome home.

Acknowledgments

Mama, look at me! I wrote a book. Well, I sure wish my dad was here still, but I suspect he knows he's being honored. I give thanks to Aunt Gail, Uncle Johnny and Aunt Jennifer, cousins Laurin and April, and the rest of my family who have believed in me and offered support through this whole process. I honor my grandmothers Alma and Doris, grandfathers Oscar and Grover (Jobe), and our ancestors who had the good sense to make their way to San Antonio, Texas—where my story began.

Love and gratitude to my mentor, Dr. Savitri Dixon-Saxon, who got this whole thing started with, "Now if I was Stacee, I'd write a book." I appreciate Drs. Stephanie J.W. Ford and Tiffany Rush-Wilson, who with my best friend Dr. Jason Patton joined me to start presenting Otherness to our students. Thanks especially to my students and clients over these many years—you all helped shape me and make me a better human.

A big shout-out to my agent, Regina Ryan, who never gave up on me, and to the *fabulous* crew at New Harbinger: Jennifer Holder, Georgia Kolias, and Vicraj Gill, your insane amount of work editing this book made it sparkle like a drag queen.

Finally, thanks to my big, brassy family-of-choice for supporting me through all this. It sure did take a village to keep your girl writing, but it's how we do.

References

Clance, P. R. and S. A. Imes. 1978. "The impostor phenomenon in high achieving women: Dynamics and therapeutic intervention." *Psychotherapy: Theory, Research, and Practice*, 15(3), 241–247.

Eisenberger, N., M. Lieberman, and K. D. Williams. 2003. October 10. "Does Rejection Hurt? An fMRI Study of Social Exclusion." *Science*, 302, 290–292.

Indian Law Resource Center. 2020. "Ending Violence Against Native Women." Accessed August 17. https://indianlaw.org/issue/ending-violence-against-native-women.

Kashdan, T. B., J. D. Elhai, and W. E. Breen. 2008. "Social anxiety and disinhibition: An analysis of curiosity and social rank appraisals, approach-avoidance conflicts, and disruptive risk-taking behavior." *Journal of Anxiety Disorders*, 22, 925–939.

Low, Rachel S. T., N. C. Overall, M. D. Hammond, and Y. U. Girme. 2017. "Emotional Suppression During Personal Goal Pursuit Impedes Goal Strivings and Achievement." *Emotion*, 17, no. 2, March, 208–23.

Miller, J. B. and I. P. Stiver. 1997. *The Healing Connection: How Women Form Relationships in Therapy and in Life.* Boston: Beacon Press.

Reicherzer, S. 2016. "What Are You Looking At?" *Family Circle*, June.

Richards, J. M., and J. J. Gross. 1999. "Composure at any cost? The cognitive consequences of emotion suppression." *Personality and Social Psychology Bulletin*, 25, 1033–1044.

Shapiro, F. 2001. *Eye Movement Desensitization and Reprocessing.* New York: Guilford Press.

Sleegers, W., T. Proulx, and I. Van Beest. 2016. "The Social Pain of Cyberball: Decreased Pupillary Reactivity to Exclusion Cues." *Journal of Experimental Social Psychology*, 69.

Webb, T. L., E. Miles, and P. Sheeran. 2012. "Dealing with feeling: a meta-analysis of the effectiveness of strategies derived from the process model of emotion regulation." *Psychological Bulletin*, 138, 775.

Reading Group Guide

Hey, fabulous reader! It's me, Stacee. I am glad you're taking time to read the book. You can deepen self-exploration and connect with each other through the power of group discussion. Here is an assortment of questions and activities to help nudge this along. Group is powerful, as you'll soon experience.

To accommodate your needs as a reading group, I've arranged each chapter's questions and prompts so they move from a more cognitive realm, for example a question about your life history, to deeper and more exploratory questions that can help you reach out and ask group members for support. They can help you make a change, identify a growth area, or give voice to a part of you that has been silenced. Choose the questions that align with what your group wants to focus on and the amount of time you have to devote to each chapter.

I hope this guide brings about very fruitful discussions!

Chapter 1: A Kid Who Was "Different"

1.   When was the first time you were cast out as Other?

2.   What were the circumstances?

3.   What did you start to believe about yourself, as a result of that experience?

4.   How was this first experience with Otherness compounded by later experiences of being outcast, bullied, or otherwise mistreated for your "difference"?

As a follow-up to individual sharing, group members may explore the impact of being a witness to each other's stories. Use these prompts to facilitate the group experience.

5.   As you told your story, what was it like to be seen?

6. What was it like hearing other people in the group describe their experiences with Otherness?

7. Reflect on talking about this experience in such an open way, with this particular group of people.

Chapter 2: What Rejection Does to Us

1. Circling back to the story you told for the chapter 1 discussion, how did you learn to deal with experiences of rejection in life?

2. What were your most common strategies for avoiding rejection?

3. What did you lose, gain, and learn from living with these strategies?

4. In what circumstances do you use these strategies for dealing with rejection today?

5. Think for a moment about rejection sensitivity: the experience of both anticipating rejection and feeling it acutely when it happens. Walk the group through a more recent scenario where this occurred, sharing as much as you feel safe to discuss. What was the backstory, and how did it lead you to anticipate rejection? What was the outcome? Were you in fact rejected, or reading your own storyline in someone's intention? If you're unsure, perhaps the group can help you gain clarity.

Chapter 3: Gathering Your Tools for the Journey to Freedom

1. In what life situation have you made a very big, deliberate choice to be free of something or someone that was harming you? Describe the journey you took, from the initial fear that held you in place to the decision you made to become free of this person or situation. Where did doing this ultimately lead you?

2. In what situation do you currently feel most stuck, yearning to be free?

3. Describe a time when you experienced clarity that seemed particularly free of mindchatter and clutter. You might recall this as a deeply spiritual experience, or one that was simply very still and profound.

4. What's one life area where you've struggled to give yourself compassion? Is there a part of you needing some forgiveness and acceptance right now?

5. How have you used creativity in the past to help you focus your energy and solve a life problem? Alternatively, have you struggled to find your creative voice? If so, what can the group offer you now to help this voice be expressed?

6. How comfortable are you with being sassy and talking back to the negative self-talk that keeps you feeling down about yourself? What do you view as drawbacks to being bold and sassy? What are the benefits that sass can bring to your life?

7. Have additional tools of change effectively helped you overcome life obstacles? Can you use them now to address experiences of Otherness in your life?

Chapter 4: "You Shouldn't Complain Because Others Are Worse Off Than You"

1. What role has this rule played in your life?

2. If you're able, pinpoint the foundation for this rule. Was there a specific person who told you that you shouldn't complain? Perhaps it was implied?

3. Have you been shamed or blamed for a problem you were attempting to voice that represented a legitimate grievance?

4. What is your relationship with pity? How has it shaped your interactions with people who use pity—intentionally or inadvertently—in a way that reinforces your Otherness?

5. What was the cost of pretending that you weren't hurting when, in fact, you were?

6. Are there life grievances related to your Otherness that you'd like to voice for the group to hear?

7. Is there a part of your story that you have tried to push away and deflect, which now needs to be grieved? What do you need from the group in order to feel seen in your grief?

Chapter 5: "You'd Better Tone It Down"

1. In what areas of your life were you told to "tone it down?"

2. How was this rule of fear delivered to you? When you attempted to be in the world in a more natural state, what were the results?

3. Describe the box that you were expected to exist in as a toned-down individual. You might think of the social roles that came with this expectation—maybe even a role within your family that seemed scripted by someone else.

4. A core message in this rule of fear is that an aspect of you, or perhaps many aspects, are fundamentally incorrect. What was it like to carry a sense of incorrectness: the message that you are not okay as you are?

5. When we follow a script that society writes for us, there are often losses as well as "rewards" that the dominant group defines for us. What has the dominant culture, even in your own family, offered you to incentivize "knowing your place" or otherwise staying within the role they defined?

6. What losses have you incurred thanks to the dominant culture's script for you and your life?

7. What part of you that's been toned down needs to be given voice now? What can the group do to support your growth, to see and support you, as you need to show up in the room right now? Then consider sharing this part with the group.

8. Is there an ancestral story that needs to be voiced to the group? Tell the story as vividly as you can. You might even introduce yourself as the person ("My name is Rojelio and I work in a mine outside of Bogotá"), telling a story from your ancestor's life as you understand it from within their perspective.

9. If you know little or nothing of your actual ancestral line, you can construct a story based on something you share with the historical person. LGBTQ+ folk might, for example, find it useful to tell the story of someone who was persecuted in the struggle for rights and acceptance. You can also embody this in the first person ("My name is Marsha P. Johnson and I'm here to tell my story about what led up to the Stonewall uprising").

10. Consider what this ancestor would want for you to be doing right now. Think of actions that they could not take and choices that were inaccessible to them. Allow the group to help you shape ways you can live the freedom they could not have.

Chapter 6: "You Must Work Twice as Hard"

1. In what area of your life do you primarily work twice as hard?

2. What keeps you believing you must work twice as hard to prove your worth, however "worth" is being measured? Is it an institution or a person?

3. What have you gained from all your work?

4. What have you sacrificed along the way?

5. Is there a distinct pattern to the ways you work twice as hard, in relationships, professional life, or other parts of your experience?

6. What is the hook that people use to convince you that you must work twice as hard?

7. Describe a time when you refused to exhaust yourself. Maybe you established boundaries for your time and resources, or you took a relaxing vacation to completely unwind. Walk the group through the biggest challenges you faced when asserting your refusal.

8. What statements about your rights need to be heard right now? Share what you are wanting and needing with the group. Just naming an experience, like exhaustion or resentment, can be particularly helpful.

9. It's easy to look back and regret past choices about what you did, or didn't, do. Is there something from your past that you'd like the group to help you move beyond?

Chapter 7: "Oh, You Shouldn't Feel Resentful!"

1. Within your story of being Othered, who or what do you resent most? Perhaps tell a story to illustrate a person or situation from your past that you resent.

2. What were you taught about resentment toward people who enjoy a level of privilege that you do not? Were you shamed or scolded for feeling resentful? Or were you expected to pretend you weren't experiencing it?

3. What do you resent most now? How and when does this resentment tend to show up for you?

4. What do you sense your resentment is trying to tell you about what you're needing but not getting in your present life?

5. In the book, we explored the story of Ernest, a man who grew up being targeted, isolated, and socially shamed by his teachers, peers, and even his parents. Ernest's old resentment showed up in many different parts of his adult life. Is there rage you also feel

that seems to come out at unrelated times? As you feel comfortable, ask the group to help you connect the dots on disowned anger and previous experiences with Othering.

6. What role do you wish resentment to play as you move forward with your life? Does it need to be channeled into something proactive, like a social change effort or a personal life change? Could it be applied to art or another creative endeavor?

7. Is there a situation you have the power to change in ways that will allow you to resent less? If old resentments exist in your personal life, invite the group to help you identify and perhaps role-play difficult dialogues that might need to happen with folks you resent.

8. Reflecting on your ancestral story, is there a particular hardship they endured that you now find yourself resenting?

9. Where can this resentment of ancestral trauma lead you so that it doesn't fester and ultimately sink you? What can you do, say, or be?

Chapter 8: "You Cannot Change the World"

1. Is there a time when you felt like an imposter? What situation had you believing that you were not truly qualified to be there? This can be from any life area: parenting, workplace, school, and more.

2. What types of behaviors do you tend to demonstrate when operating from a belief that you're a phony, an imposter? What do you do or don't do, say or don't say?

3. When you felt this imposter role in one area of life, what was the impact that it had on your other life areas?

4. Self-sabotage comes when we fear our own success or the changes that accomplishment could bring. Is there a pattern to your self-sabotage? What role has self-sabotage played in your life?

5. What did you sabotage when you were in a state of pain from being Othered?

6. Think about the role of despair in your life, and how it's connected to ongoing experiences of Othering. What issues cause you to revisit your despair?

7. What coping strategies have you used, successfully or unsuccessfully, to address Otherness despair in your life?

8. In the activities for this chapter, you read Chinh's sample letter to himself, and wrote one to yourself. Would you feel safe sharing what you wrote with the group? If so, allow yourself to be witnessed by reading the letter out loud.

9. You described your "rock" in your journal, which you plan to use for addressing despair in your life. As you feel comfortable, share the rock story with the group.

10. Are there elements of this group that can serve as a rock for members in the times to come?

Chapter 9: Weaken the Internal Oppressor's Stranglehold on Your Voice

1. What current circumstances are happening in the world that seem particularly demoralizing, if not devastating, for you?

2. How has your story of addressing Otherness in your life prepared you for dealing with present realities?

3. Describe your internal oppressor to the group. Whose voice does it use—your own or someone else's? Perhaps its voice originated with a particularly oppressive person in your past or present.

4. What situations feed your internal oppressor? When is its "feeding time"—do you feed it at night with a lot of hurtful thoughts when you should be sleeping instead? Or in daytime by staying glued to negative newsfeeds and social media?

5. What actions have you taken in the past that weakened your internal oppressor? Perhaps distill this into a specific story you'd like to share with the group.

6. We can refuse to isolate. What is this group giving you that's allowed you to break free from isolation and the negative thought spirals that tend to accompany it?

7. What did you learn about your internal oppressor from the exercises in this chapter? What was it like to dialogue with this part of you?

8. We all need a personal judgement-free zone. Is there anything this group could do right now that would help it feel like a judgement-free zone?

Chapter 10: Finding Your Way Home Through Community

1. What are your intersections that are central to your identity as a racial, cultural, gendered, sexual, spiritual being?

2. What is the hardest part about finding and building community with people? Was it tougher than expected with those who share a connection or identity? What is the most rewarding part of being in community?

3. How has your journey gone to find people who, like you, are seeking growth and change for themselves?

4. Consider the role that growth-fostering relationships have played to move you from Other to a place of community and connection. Who or what comes to mind as particularly helpful? Perhaps

share a story with the group about a particular connection that has allowed you to feel less Othered.

5. What relationships exist for you right now that are toxic, perhaps by perpetuating the rules of fear in your life?

6. How have you established boundaries or distanced yourself so these people do not harm you with their mess? Is this something the group might help you with? If so, ask for what you need.

7. What did you experience during the process of offering compassionate healing to people around you—to those you love, strangers around the globe, ancestors, a person you Othered. Were some aspects easier or more difficult than others?

Closing Compassion Activity

I want to suggest a final activity, because the closing work in the book included the practice of extending compassion to larger and larger circles of people. Your group can create a circle of compassion. Here are steps for doing this.

Assign a group member to organize the group and serve as the leader. This person will direct the group on when to carry out essential parts of the exercises and organize you so that you're sitting directly across from another person. When the time comes, you need to be able to gaze at the other person. Here are instructions for the group leader to share.

- Bring yourselves into a shared meditative space by simply dropping your gazes to the floor, or closing your eyes altogether, and assuming comfortable sitting positions.

- Allow yourself to breathe, taking in each breath through the nose and exhaling out through the mouth.

- If you have interrupting thoughts, that's okay. Just label them "thinking." And continue with your breath. Do this clarity exercise for three to five minutes.

- Afterward, raise your gaze to the person directly in front of you. Make eye contact. Continue your breath. Witness the person in their story, as you've come to know it. Breathe in their story, their experience of hurt. And breathe out healing energy, love, radiance, abundance, and other things you recognize the other person may be needing. Allow this to continue for the next few minutes.

- Then come back together with the larger group. Invite members to process what the experience was like as they gave and received compassion.

Stacee L. Reicherzer, PhD, is a Chicago, IL-based transgender counselor, educator, and public speaker for the stories of the bullied, forgotten, and oppressed. The San Antonio, TX, native serves as clinical faculty of counseling at Southern New Hampshire University, where she received the distinguished faculty award in 2018. She travels the globe to teach and engage audiences around diverse topics of Otherness, self-sabotage, and imposter phenomenon.

Real change *is* possible

For more than forty-five years, New Harbinger has published proven-effective self-help books and pioneering workbooks to help readers of all ages and backgrounds improve mental health and well-being, and achieve lasting personal growth. In addition, our spirituality books offer profound guidance for deepening awareness and cultivating healing, self-discovery, and fulfillment.

Founded by psychologist Matthew McKay and Patrick Fanning, New Harbinger is proud to be an independent, employee-owned company. Our books reflect our core values of integrity, innovation, commitment, sustainability, compassion, and trust. Written by leaders in the field and recommended by therapists worldwide, New Harbinger books are practical, accessible, and provide real tools for real change.

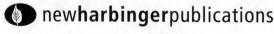 **newharbinger**publications

MORE BOOKS from
NEW HARBINGER PUBLICATIONS

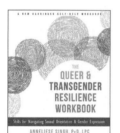

Register your **new harbinger** titles for additional benefits!

When you register your **new harbinger** title—purchased in any format, from any source—you get access to benefits like the following:

- Downloadable accessories like printable worksheets and extra content

- Instructional videos and audio files

- Information about updates, corrections, and new editions

Not every title has accessories, but we're adding new material all the time.

Access free accessories in 3 easy steps:

1. Sign in at NewHarbinger.com (or **register** to create an account).

2. Click on **register a book**. Search for your title and click the **register** button when it appears.

3. Click on the **book cover or title** to go to its details page. Click on **accessories** to view and access files.

That's all there is to it!

If you need help, visit:

NewHarbinger.com/accessories

new harbinger
CELEBRATING
40 YEARS